ABOUT THE AUTHOR

Marites A. Khanser, DBA was formerly a permanent, full time faculty with a rank of Full Professor for eight years under the School of Business and Economic (SBE) of the University of San Carlos (USC), in Cebu City, Philippines. Dr. Khanser recently won for her team the **Best Idea Award 2017-2018**, a prestigious award from IDE Accelerator 2018 Program of Thailand and MIT-Boston for their product idea on developing a perpetual lighting system using bioluminescence. She is also an author of several books, especially, the business biography of John L. Gokongwei, Jr., a Filipino-Chinese taipan in the Philippines, titled, John L. Gokongwei, Jr.: The Path of Entrepreneurship (Khanser, 2007), published by the Ateneo de Manila University.

Dr. Khanser finished a Doctor of Business Administration (DBA) from the De La Salle University (DLSU), Manila, Philippines, in 1998. She is an international researcher, a book author, and a Management Consultant to industry clients.

ABOUT THE AUTHOR

Soontorn Piromsartkoon, B.Eng, M.EEM, MBA, DBA, has an Engineering Management Background and currently holds the position of the President of Mentor Management and Consultant Company located in Thailand. This company is well known for a consulting of engineering and management in Thailand and is into promoting it to the global market as well. He is a specialist in the field of Civil Engineering and Environment Engineering and Management from Asian Institute of Technology (AIT).

Dr. Soontorn has started to do research and writing a book and has worked together with Dr. Khanser during the IDE 2018 Accelerator Program of Thailand and MIT-Boston for the bioluminescent perpetual lighting start up.

In addition, Dr. Soontorn works also as Chief Executive Officer and Chief Marketing Officer for Toechok Company Limited, Thailand of www.toechok.com that provides a tourism network in the form of a web platform.

PRAISES FROM OUR READERS:

It is my pleasure to endorse this book to everyone as an excellent reading material for a general understanding of bioluminescence and the creatures of light. I am happy to note the collaboration of two authors coming from two Asian countries: the Philippines and Thailand. This is a clear indication that Asian inventors and innovators are making their mark in the field of science and technology.

My heartfelt congratulations to the authors, Dr. Marites A. Khanser and Dr. Soontorn Piromsartkoon, for the excellent publication of this book.

— **Professor Worsak Kanok-Nukulchai, Ph.D (UC Berkeley)**
President, Asian Institute of Technology (AIT), Bangkok, Thailand

Congratulations to Dr. Marites Khanser and Dr. Soontorn Piromsartkoon, her Co-Inventor. The Philvencap is with both of you in your journey to success. We wish you both all the best!

— **Mr. Edmundo Isidro**
President, Philippine Venture Capital Investment Group (Philvencap)
Asian Institute of Management (AIM), Makati City, Philippines

You have a great mind, Ma'am Tess. Cheering you and Soontorn on to greater heights in the path you've chosen.

— **Lauro Cipriano R. Silapan, Jr., DBA**
Coordinator, Graduate Programs, School of Business & Economics
University of San Carlos, Cebu City, Philippines

PRAISES FROM OUR READERS:

If the perpetual bioluminescent lighting system of Dr. Marites A. Khanser and Dr. Soontorn Piromsartkoon will become commercially viable, they will be making a great contribution to science and industry. If they succeed, the perpetual bioluminescent lighting product will be the first product to be commercialized using bioluminescence as source of light.

— Anchana Thancharoen, PhD
Entomologist, Department of Entomology
Faculty of Agriculture, Kasetsart University
Bangkok, Thailand

When the authors challenge the reader to use their imagination to come up with new ideas that may lead to new inventions, then proceed to cite examples of some "crazy" ideas that have or may soon have commercial application, the reader begins to think of going beyond his/her comfort zone. This call to imaginative thinking and action is in my opinion one of the greatest values of this book.

— Milagros Guerrero Barretto
Former Faculty, College of Business Administration
University of the Philippines
Diliman, Quezon City, Philippines

BIOLUMINESCENT LIGHT

A Disruptive Innovation
of the Future

BIOLUMINESCENT LIGHT

A Disruptive Innovation
of the Future

Marites A. Khanser & **Soontorn Piromsartkoon**

บริษัท เมนเทอร์ เมเนจเมนท์ คอนซัลแตนท์ จำกัด
MENTOR MANAGEMENT CONSULTANT CO.,LTD.
14 navamin 98 khannayaow Bangkok Thailand 10230
publication@mentormanagements.com
URL: www.mentormanagements.com

Published by:
Mentor Management Consultant Company (MMC), Ltd
14 navamin 98 khannayaow Bangkok Thailand 10230
publication@mentormanagements.com
URL: www.mentormanagements.com

Cover Design Artist: **Brendon Baclaan**
Layout Artist: **Edik Dolotina**
Editor: **Br. Romualdo Abulad, SVD**
Information Technologist: **Namchok Petsaen**

ISBN 978-616-93122-2-2

This book is dedicated to all the inventors and innovators of the world:

may your tribe grow

PROLOGUE

On November 26, 2017, the Team Perpetual Light Biotechnologies were admitted to the IDE 2018 Accelerator Program of Thailand and MIT-Boston as Fellows, and it was there in Thailand that we won the Best Idea Award and a monetary prize for our product idea on developing a perpetual lighting system using bioluminescence.

Winning that prestigious award gave us the confidence for the business potential of the project that we submitted. We were very earnest to achieve our goal in the coming months. At the same time, we decided to create a theme on bioluminescence for this book with our passion to inform our readers all over the world so that they will know how to transform the technologies of electrical lighting into a perpetual bioluminescent lighting system, which is considered a disruptive innovation of the future.

We firmly believe that if you pick up and read our book you will be very excited about what Steve Jobs said, "The biggest innovation of the twenty-first century will be the intersection of technology and biology. A new era is beginning." Indeed, our book will show you the way biotechnology and synthetic biology can enable you to think of inventions that you have never imagined before and so become a part of this new era.

The power of your imagination will enable you to navigate well the Industry 4.0, a new economic engine that will transform the way you live, the way you think, and the way you create and innovate.

Imagine what our world will be by 2025, driven by the Fourth Industrial Revolution – driven by technologies. That world belongs to you, our young readers, and the possibilities of such a world will depend on your capacity to take up a BIG dream and make it a reality. Think BIG, but act small. This is the wisdom shared to us by our dear mentors and coaches of the IDE Accelerator.

You will need great passion and confidence to take part in Industry 4.0; you need to be much, much better than the robots of the future that will surpass your human intelligence. The challenge of Artificial Intelligence or AI is before you: be enslaved by it, or conquer it and be its master.

We are confident that you will choose to be the master of these artificial machines. There is a secret that we would like to let you in, a secret found in our book, and it is this: Robots cannot match your leaps of intelligence and the power of imagination that you are capable of, nor can Artificial Intelligence be a match to your capacity to evolve as spiritual beings with the capacity to love and be loved; the ability to dream and pursue this dream relentlessly until you make it into reality. Always remember what Einstein believed in, "Imagination is more important than knowledge."

Lastly, we know that our world today and in the foreseeable future needs to engage in environmental protection. In the song composed by one of the authors of this book, Dr. Soontorn Piromsartkoon, titled "*A Beautiful World*", he sings of "*a beautiful world where rain forests abound, and where animals roam free, and the people live in harmony together and free and love one another.*" And the song's message is for us to stop destroying the only world we have. We provide you a copy of this song which we hope would inspire you to take part in saving our Planet, so that you will commit yourself to the task of maintaining our beautiful world today for the future of generations to come.

CONTENTS

FOREWORD

It was with delight that I accepted the invitation to write a Foreword for the book, titled, *Bioluminescent Light: A Disruptive Innovation of the Future* (Khanser and Piromsartkoon, 2018). When I was approached by Dr. Soontorn Piromsartkoon for this task, I was intrigued by the topic of the book. The phenomenon of bioluminescence has been with us for quite a long time now and one thing that reminds me of it is the light of the fireflies. What is amazing about the book is that it features the Khanser-Piromsartkoon invention of a perpetual lighting system using bioluminescence which they present as a disruptive innovation of the future, something that will challenge our current understanding of lighting systems. The invention is an alternative green energy and uses synthetic biology to produce the bioluminescent light.

The book attempts to provide an in-depth analysis of bioluminescence as a possible source of light. The technology still belongs to the frontiers of science and it is at the intersection between technology and biology, thus, biotechnology. The Industrial Revolution 4.0 includes among other cutting-edge innovations, biotechnology, and in particular, synthetic biology. The Khanser-Piromsartkoon disruptive innovation is pioneering and a very important contribution to the search for renewable energy for environmental protection.

The possible commercialization of bioluminescent perpetual lighting system will be a welcome innovative product in the global market. It will provide light to 20% of the world population that have no access to electricity. It is my pleasure to endorse this book to everyone as an excellent reading material for a general understanding of bioluminescence and the creatures of light. I am happy to note the collaboration of two authors coming from two Asian countries: the Philippines and Thailand. This is a clear indication that Asian inventors and innovators are making their mark in the field of science and technology.

My heartfelt Congratulations to the authors, Dr. Marites A. Khanser and Dr. Soontorn Piromsartkoon for the excellent publication of this book.

Professor Worsak Kanok-Nukulchai, Ph.D (UC Berkeley)
President, Asian Institute of Technology (AIT)
Bangkok, Thailand
April, 2018

FOREWORD

Dr. Marites Khanser made a presentation on her project, Natural Light Biotechnologies/Bioluminescent Light, last October 26, 2017 to the Philippine Venture Capital Investment Group (Philvencap). The subject matter of her project was unheard of in the forum and the concept was difficult to comprehend. However, to her credit, as she continued to make her presentation and within a span of 5 minutes, many people among the audience noticed her confidence, her passion and the ingenuity of her concept.

I met her again in another forum at the Asian Institute of Management (AIM), during the Master of Science in Innovation and Business (MIB) program Demo Day, where many highly technical projects were also being presented. Again, her interest, passion and enthusiasm in looking at other projects and trying to meet people who could help her fund her project was very evident.

Ultimately, she went to Thailand as she was selected to join the IDE Accelerator 2018 Program of Thailand and MIT-Boston and it was there that she won the Best Idea Award and a monetary prize.

The Philvencap is glad she first made her presentation to this forum whose primary aim is to provide budding entrepreneurs a chance to present their projects before business angels and other private individuals who could be interested in financing the projects to enable them to build a prototype and bring this to market.

The Philvencap was organized in April 1987 and subsequently went into partnership with AIM through the efforts of the AIM President at that time, Prof. Felipe B. Alfonso. The recent thrust of AIM under the new leadership of President & Dean Jikyeong Kang has been further strengthened by AIM's new trajectory of program innovation and expansion further aligning itself to the demands of an emerging Asia towards the digital age.

The forum has continued to work very closely with AIM for 25 years now and gives opportunities to entrepreneurs, including students, to make project presentations before a live interested, investing audience. We nurture new entrepreneurs and the forum serves as "first blood drawn" when they present before the live audience. The Philvencap serves as a cog in the ecosystem for new ideas, new projects and new entrepreneurs.

Congratulations to Dr. Marites Khanser and Dr. Soontorn Piromsartkoon, her Co-Inventor. The Philvencap is with both of you in your journey to success. We wish you both all the best!

Mr. Edmundo Isidro
President, Philippine Venture Capital Investment
Group (Philvencap)
Asian Institute of Management (AIM)
Makati City, Philippines
January, 2018

INTRODUCTION

When I started researching for references on bioluminescence written for general readership, I could not find one available in the book market. I discussed with Dr. Soontorn Piromsartkoon to make a startup product on a bioluminescent light and we started to propose the product idea to IDE 2018 Accelerator Program of Thailand and MIT-Boston, USA, and we were selected as Fellows. At the same time, we started writing this book on bioluminescent light as a disruptive innovation of the future.

For the past thirty years of my life, an idea has been brewing in my mind and continued to persist despite the passage of time. It was the idea of coming up with a street lighting system mimicking the light produced by the firefly. At that time, I consulted Dr. Soontorn on this invention. And we started to do research together because we considered it very important to mimic the bioluminescent light in the future.

Based on our research, we have finally come to an understanding of how the firefly produces the bioluminescent light. The technology is now available and it is only a matter of time that our product idea will become an invention that can change our current concept of lighting systems.

Today, there might be others in the world who are working on a similar invention. It is a race for us on who will be the first to make bioluminescent lighting system as a commercial product. Such efforts may earn for the inventor/s a future Nobel Prize.

We decided to write this book to provide the basic concepts of bioluminescence. The book is divided into six parts, namely:

Part 1 – *On Climate Change and Green Energy.* This section provides an overview of the current concerns about climate change, environmental protection, and the search for alternative energy, in particular, green energy and how bioluminescent lighting system can provide a solution.

Part 2 – *The Dream and the Imagination.* This looks back to the 30–year journey since the birth of the product idea and its relation to Biomimicry, and breaking through the cloud of unknowing.

Part 3 – *On the Phenomenon of Bioluminescence.* This is the focus of the book which is to provide the basic concepts of bioluminescence and its uses for humans. And also to explore the risks associated with biological source of light.

Part 4 – *Bioluminescent Light: Disruptive Innovation.* This section deals on the Industrial Revolution 4.0, on biotechnology and how it is changing our world, on synthetic biology and why bioluminescent lighting system is considered a disruptive innovation of the future.

Part 5 – *How Bioluminescent Light will Benefit the World.* This section deals on the benefits of using Bioluminescent Lighting System and other benefits that the innovation offers such as environmental protection, health protection, a source of alternative energy, a solution to reducing carbon footprint, as well as enjoying the miracles of biotechnologies.

Part 6 – *Inventions for the Next 50 Years.* To have a useful ending to this book, we added some possible inventions for the next 50 years. Most importantly, we would like to emphasize that the use of biotechnology, or other types of technology, like artificial intelligence, should be in the service of furthering human spiritual evolution; that we are spiritual beings and no machine can match our leaps of intelligence.

We invite our readers to join us in this exciting journey of scientific discovery and the exploration of the uses of disruptive innovations that still belong to the frontiers of science, and hence, the future.

Marites A. Khanser, DBA
Author
Cebu City, Philippines
June, 2018

INTRODUCTION

I am happy that Dr. Khanser and I collaboratively work on the start up on the bioluminescent light and a very good opportunity to push the project in the Asian soil. First of all, I would like to thank IDE for giving me the chance to explore new technologies through the intersection of technology and biology. At the same time, I talked to Dr. Khanser that we must write a book for bioluminescent light as a disruptive innovation of the future. This is in order that the readers of the world will understand more about bioluminescence as a part of green energy and that it is possible to produce a commercial product in the future.

According to my expertise and as I plotted the idea and as I discussed with Dr. Khanser, we decided to create a theme for the book with our passion to inform our readers all over the world so they will know how to transform the technologies of electrical lighting into perpetual bioluminescent lighting.

We divide the book into six parts and we started to write together.

I would like to emphasize that we live in a world where we humans are enjoying the products and services of advanced technology, and yet we are faced with growing concerns for the disastrous effects of environmental damage and global climate change due to global warming. As a consequence, there is the melting of the giant glaciers in Antarctica and in the North Pole which is expected to raise the sea level and natural disasters through hurricanes, typhoons, flooding, and earthquakes.

In the comforts of our modern life, made available to us by science and technology, all these seem remote. Yet, when natural disasters strike with a great force that destroy plants and animals, and most especially people, we then realize that Mother Earth is not such a safe planet anymore.

We believe that in writing this book, we will be able to reach out to millions of our readers across the globe and send our message of hope for the future of mankind and an optimism that springs from our knowledge that we can positively engage in environmental protection. Many of us are in search of alternative means to reduce our carbon footprint and are following the green path. In our case, we propose a green energy – an alternative lighting system that will use bioluminescence that comes naturally from fireflies and some sea creatures like the squid, the jelly fish, and the glowworms, among others. It is the topic on bioluminescence on which this book is particularly focused. This alternative source of light has no carbon footprint.

As of this writing, we continue to research and look for all possible ways to develop our prototype of the bioluminescent perpetual lighting system, inspired by the firefly.

I had the opportunity to interview an Entomologist from Thailand, Dr. Anchana Thancharoen, who is an expert on fireflies, who shared with us her research findngs for her 16 years of study on fireflies. We also sought help from Dr. Edith Widder from Florida, USA, world expert on bioluminescence and who generously provided us her valuable article on marine bioluminescence. We would like to encourage our readers to continue to engage in the dialogue with us on how the bioluminescent light can be put to good use.

We invite you to read our book and be aware of how the phenomenon of bioluminescence can be harnessed as a source of alternative light. The natural world has a lot to teach us. It is through Biomimicry that we can make innovations inspired by nature.

Let us learn from nature for the sustainability of Planet Earth.

Soontorn Piromsartkoon, DBA
Author
Bangkok, Thailand
June, 2018

PART ONE

On Climate Change and Green Energy

CHAPTER 1

The Global Climate Change and Why we Should Worry

Environmental damage as a result of man's activities that disregard environmental protection should be a great concern for humankind. We are experiencing natural disasters because our planet is getting warmer and our climate is changing. What climate change has done for our environment is staggering to think about. We have air and ocean getting warmer because sea level is rising, and our ocean is becoming more acidic. Because carbon dioxide (i.e. carbon emission) reacts with water in oceans and seas to form carbonic acid, so the ocean becomes acidic. This results in the further warming of the bodies of water. The huge glaciers and ice sheets in Greenland and Antarctica are shrinking, meaning, that they are melting at a fast rate because of global warming, and this is causing the sea level to rise. A worst scenario for the next 50 years would be that most of our cities in the world might go underwater. Future generations may have to live submerged in water, a future hard to contemplate, but very likely to happen.

Global climate change is a complex issue and we should understand why we should worry. But first we need to understand the difference between climate change and ozone depletion. When we speak of ozone depletion, we need to go back to our basic knowledge of our sun. The sun produces visible light as well as other forms of light or radiation, invisible to the naked eye.

According to Hoffman (1998), "to either side of the spectrum of visible light, it has the ultraviolet light (UV) and infrared light, also called radiant heat." He pointed out further that the problem of ozone depletion concerns the effects of UV light. However, the problem of greenhouse effect or global warming concerns the effects of visible and infrared light. There are some alarming facts we should also know about these lights from the sun (Hoffman, 1998). Two of these are:

1. UV light, if unfiltered, is very damaging to the biological tissue; and

2. When visible light strikes an object, it warms it up, then the warm object radiates infrared light, or heat. The earth atmosphere acts as filter and insulator.

Why should this worry us? In essence, we can summarize the difference between ozone depletion and climate change as follows: Ozone depletion allows more ultraviolet light through the atmosphere; the greenhouse effect warms the planet because the atmosphere passes visible light through the earth's surface, but greenhouse gases block some of the resulting radiant heat from getting away (Hoffman, 1998). It is worrisome because these two phenomena, ozone depletion and global warming, are causing negative effects to our environment.

Increases in greenhouse effect are referred to as global warming or global climate change. This is our main concern for today. We are faced with increasing problems of natural disasters such as flooding, typhoons, earthquakes, storm surges, hurricanes, tsunami, and widespread damage to marine ecosystems, among others.

Today, countries, businesses and individuals are faced with increasing pressure for reducing greenhouse gas emissions, such as carbon dioxide, methane and nitrous oxide, in response to climate change. Governments have taken an active stance in dealing with environmental issues as early as the late 1970s leading towards the creation of the Intergovernmental Panel on Climate Change and the drafting of the Kyoto Protocol (UNFCCC, 2003).

Indeed, climate change has become a major issue globally as efforts to reduce carbon emissions become urgent to protect Mother Earth from further environmental havoc. The authorities in the field are now promoting new market-based mechanisms in Asian countries and contributing global efforts to combat climate change. The UNFCCC considers greenhouse gas (GHG) emissions as a new commodity since emitting a set limit (set by Kyoto Protocol in 1997) entails a potential cost to companies.

Ratnunga remarked that the rapid climate change calls for greater attention to "carbon management in the decision-making process" (Ratnunga, 2008, p. 1). The author pointed out that there is very little literature available in scholarly journals that focused on the impact of carbon trading on carbon emission reduction initiatives. Hence, there is a need for strategic management accounting techniques and measures in order to address pressing issues on trading in carbon allowances (carbon credits) and investment in low-carbon emission technologies, among others. She calls this new carbon economic environment as "carbonomics". Furthermore, the author noted that the key issue of mandatory carbon rationing and trading schemes "may affect business strategies, financial performance, and organizational value."

Climate change mitigation offers solutions to address the global climate change. It has to be recognized that climate change is a global problem that calls for international cooperation in tandem with local, national, and regional policies. Mitigation, in the context of climate change, is defined as a human intervention to reduce the sources or enhance the sinks of greenhouse gases (GHGs). It is assumed that not to take action towards mitigation would be tantamount to allowing adverse impacts to continue which directly harm humans and ecological well–beings. These activities exceed the ability of these systems to adapt adequately.

One of these mitigation approaches concerns the adoption of renewable energy. Increase in carbon emissions comes from the energy sector. We have been using fossil fuels to cope with increasing demand for electricity. And yet, 1.4 billion people in the world have no access to electricity. Renewable energy can offer solutions to reduce carbon footprint in the manufacturing sector. The renewable energy identified in the IPCC paper consists of bio-energy, direct solar energy, geothermal energy, hydropower, ocean energy, and wind energy. It is on the area of bio-energy that we would like to focus in this book.

We move on to the importance of searching for an alternative Green Energy aside from biomass.

Interview with the executives of Thanakorn Vegetable Oil Products Co., Ltd, Thailand on their carbon footprint. With the authors (Dr. Soontorn and Dr. Khanser) is the company President, Mr. Adul Premprasert. With the authors is also another researcher, Concepcion Racaza. Photo provided by Thanakorn staff. This interview is part of a research funded by London-based CIMA (Chartered Institute of Management Accountants).

CHAPTER 2

On Reducing Carbon Footprint

In December of 2015, the Paris Agreement was signed by 195 countries which became the signatories to a new global agreement on climate change.

The developing countries have the reputation of having the most vulnerable populations when it comes to climate change. For instance, Asia and the Pacific have very dynamic economies but they are also the most prone to the negative impact of climate change since they have the highest incidence of greenhouse gas emissions. Most importantly, they have high carbon emissions which come from the manufacturing sector. The Paris Agreement of 2015 has agreed to lower carbon emissions up to 2% by 2020. Thus, there is a need to reduce carbon footprint, particularly in the industry sector of the society.

What is carbon footprint? Why should we worry when our activities contribute to carbon footprint? According to Chakaborty and Roy (2013), "carbon footprint" is a measure of the total amount of carbon dioxide emissions that is directly or indirectly caused by or accumulated over the life cycle stages of a product. In the manufacturing sector, there are many production activities that contribute to carbon emissions. The value of knowing a company's carbon footprint is that it helps to identify those collective consumptions and analyze which consumptions contribute significantly to greenhouse gases.

The goal is to reduce the carbon footprint in the production activities. Regarding the companies which are emitters of carbon dioxide, either they are charged with carbon tax or they avail of carbon credits in the carbon trading market. As defined, carbon trading is a market-based mechanism to mitigate climate change's negative impact. The idea is that, when a company is able to reduce its carbon emissions, it is extended carbon emission credits which then can be traded in carbon trading exchanges or in voluntary offset markets. The carbon credit works like any kind of tradeable asset. Carbon trading is one of those mechanisms by which to encourage companies to reduce their carbon footprint.

KPMG (2008) came up with an interesting report titled "Accounting for carbon: the impact of carbon trading on financial statements." The KPMG Advisory Group remarked that "accounting for carbon emissions will take many companies into new territory for which no specific accounting standard exists." (KPMG, 2008). They pointed out the following needs to consider the impact of carbon accounting: emitters, creators (or innovators of green energy), traders/brokers/aggregators, and investors/consultants. Emitters have to stay below their limits, thus the birth of carbon credits and carbon trading.

How does carbon trading work? It is interesting to point out that firms which have high GHG emissions need to pay a price per tonne of the carbon dioxide (CO2) that they are emitting in the environment. This price is called carbon price. This strategy of attaching a price to carbon emissions and creating a market to trade them is done to give incentives to those companies which have reduced their carbon footprint.

In other words, today we now have a mechanism to reward those organizations which engage in carbon emission reduction and penalize those which continue, as emitters of greenhouse gases, to have high carbon footprint.

Environmental performance indicators are described, according to Sarkis, Hervani and Helms (2005), in ISO 1403. These are needed when evaluating carbon trading and footprint. Among the instruments for measuring carbon footprint and assessment standards are the Life Cycle Analysis (LCA), Input-Output Analysis (IOA), and the Green Value Chain Analysis. Performance management can monitor the implementations of the company's plan that provides for control system (Atkinson et al., 1997).

Organizations worldwide now trade in carbon (carbon

dioxide) which is now being tracked and traded like any other commodity. There are winners and losers in the carbon trading markets. Companies buy or sell this commodity and carbon price has become highly volatile and uncertain.

Life Cycle Assessment (LCA) is a tool that can be used to evaluate the carbon emissions of a product process or activity throughout its life cycle. LCA also called Life Cycle Analysis (Cucek et al., 2012) is conventionally "characterized as a cradle-to-grave approach", as an open loop. It is a structured, comprehensive, internationally-standardized tool (environment management standards ISO 14040 and 14044, set in 2006). The LCA quantifies emissions, resource consumptions, and environmental and health impacts associated with processes, products, or activities throughout its life cycle. As an assessment tool for value chain analysis, LCA is comprised of four phases: goal and scope definition, inventory analysis, Life Impact Assessment (LIA), and interpretation.

CHAPTER 3

Green Energy

It has been observed that the energy supply sector is "the largest contributor to global GHG emissions" (Hoffert et al., 2002). The real culprit for this increase is the escalating demand for energy services. According to Hoffert et al. (2002), the annual GHG emission from the global energy supply sector has grown rapidly between 2000 and 2010, and since then it has increased steadily. The global fuel mix includes coal that releases high carbon emission as fossil fuels do.

There is therefore a need to reduce reliance on fossil fuels and shift to energy sources that do not emit carbon dioxide in the atmosphere. We call these as renewable energy, which is a part of what is called Clean Development Mechanism (CDM). The goal is to develop alternative energy that will not leave carbon footprint. These alternative energy sources can be natural or man-made.

Hoffert et al. (2002) evaluated possible future energy sources, for their capability to supply massive amounts of carbon emission–free energy and for their potential for large-scale commercialization. Possible candidates for primary energy sources include terrestrial solar and wind energy, solar power satellites, and biomass, among others. We will call them green energy.

What is a Green Energy?

How is Green Energy defined? When we talk of Green Energy, we mean an environment-friendly energy source commonly known as Renewable Energy or Sustainable Energy. The important thing to remember is that the energy comes from a natural source like wind, water, and sunlight. The green energy can be produced with little pollution, with less or no carbon footprint, so that it does not contribute to climate change or global warming like what traditional energy sources do to our environment.

The common types of green energy are the following:

Solar Energy

Solar energy is made up of cells that convert sunlight to electricity without any moving parts. The conversion of sunlight into electricity is made possible by the special properties of a semi-conducting material. Furthermore, solar energy systems do not produce air pollutants or carbon dioxide,

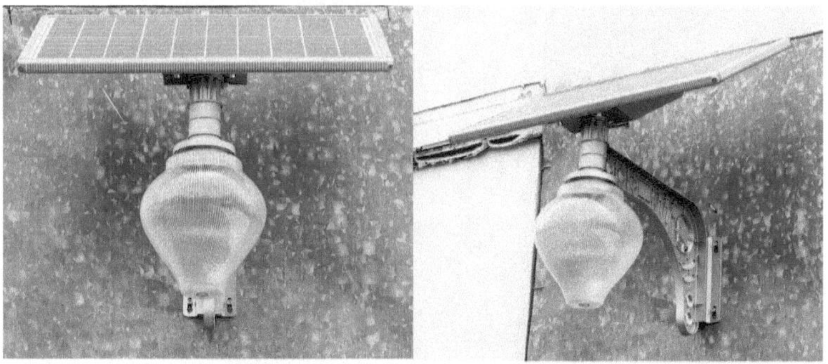

Solar panels as renewable energy. Photo taken by Dr. Soontorn Piromsartkoon, May 1, 2018.

making it a good option for those interested in lowering their carbon footprint. Solar energy can also help businesses promote their organizations as environmentally and socially responsible companies. There are many organizations now that have opted to use solar energy to reduce their electric consumption. However it must be pointed out that investing in solar panels will need initial high cost, but the depreciation is likely to last over twenty-five years. The solar users are given incentives by the government or the private sector by lowering their electric bills.

Wind Energy

Kelley (n.d.) studied wind energy, its application, limits, and potential. While it is not our desire here to discuss the technical aspects of producing wind energy, we will, however, provide a basic understanding of how wind energy is produced.

What is wind and where does it come from? It is

Windmills in Ranot, Songkhla, Thailand, as a renewable energy. Photo taken by Dr. Soontorn Piromsartkoon, May 1, 2018.

something we take for granted, just like the air we breathe. It is a natural phenomenon and we just take it as is. But wind is, according to Kelly, "caused by the energy radiated to the Earth by the sun." The beam of the radiation from the sun would heat the Earth's surface (Kelly, n.d.). When this happens, it creates temperature differences between the land, water, and air, due to their different properties, such as density, which affect their respective abilities to absorb heat (Kelly, n.d.). It is interesting to point out that all these temperature differences and different properties create what we know as wind.

Wind is defined as a "current of air (sometimes with

considerable force) from an area of high pressure to an area of low pressure." (Kelly, n.d.)

How do we harness the wind energy? Here is how Kelly (n.d.), explains the process.

Wind power is the conversion of wind energy into more useful forms. Most modern wind power is generated in the form that is produced by a wind turbine with its rotating blades that harness the wind's kinetic energy. Wind turbines contain generators that harness the mechanical energy from the spinning blades to generate electricity. A wind turbine is a rotary engine in which the kinetic energy of a moving fluid is converted into mechanical energy by causing a bladed rotor to rotate. The simplest way to think about this process is by our familiarity with the electric fan. A wind turbine works the opposite of electric fan. The turbine blades spin from the wind and make energy, instead of using energy to make a wind.

In order to have the most efficient harnessing of wind energy, it is suggested to put the turbines close together to form a wind plant. Cost considerations in investing on the turbines should be made. There is limited supply of wind energy to supply for the electricity needs of communities, and yet it is one of the renewable energies that do not have carbon footprint.

Biomass

Biomass is produced when organic wastes, such as trees, wood wastes and agriculture residues decay. For example, landfills offer a primary source of biomass. This can be converted to fuel through combustion for the generation of electricity. The resulting gas is methane and can be used as an alternative energy.

Bio-energy can be combined with carbon capture and storage. This strategy offers the prospect of large energy supply with net negative emissions. However, this stabilization scenario is not without its own challenges and risks (IPCC, 1998). Technological challenges and risks, according to IPCC, include those associated with the upstream provision of biomass.

Landfill Gas

Another renewable energy is the landfill gas produced by waste materials. If the landfill is properly engineered, then the landfill gas can be collected safely so as not to cause environmental harm and affect human health. This then can be a source of energy for the community. The gas is 60% methane gas and 40% carbon dioxide.

How is landfill gas produced? There are different processes that produce landfill gas, and these are the following;

Biodegradation. The reason for the waste segregation of our garbage nowadays is to separate the biodegradable waste from the non-biodegradable. The waste material which has organic matter in the waste such as food waste and garden waste, among others, are broken down by the action of bacteria.

Volatilisation. As we throw away our garbage in our homes, like our household and other wastes, there are many compounds and these change from solid to liquid or vapor in a landfill. The mixture of these vapors becomes the trace gas components of the landfill gas.

Chemical reactions. The chemicals in the waste can likewise produce a chemical reaction so that trace gas from landfill is produced.

The waste material that we generate ends up in landfill where it decomposes and produces a gas mode of approximately 5% methane. This gas can be captured and used to fuel electric generators. Since large landfills must burn off this gas anyway in order to reduce the hazards arising from gas buildup, this method of renewable energy is one of the most successful.

Hydroelectric Power

Hydroelectricity is one option to meet the increasing demand for energy and is considered a renewable energy source.

Relying on the water cycle, falling water, running water or ocean energy (power or waves), which may be harnessed for useful purposes, a hydroelectric power station utilizes water flow to power a turbine. The turbines are connected to generators that produce energy through the use of water currents. The amount of energy generated is determined by the speed the water flows. Therefore, a swiftly flowing river will generate more electricity than a slow moving current.

Benefits of Renewable Energy (RE) and impact on sustainable development

Finally, it should be emphasized here that the Renewable Energy (RE) approach has many benefits for the world and its contribution to sustainable development. Firstly, RE can speed up access to energy in particular for the 1.4 billion people worldwide who are without access to electricity; this comprises around 19% of the world population who are still in the dark. Of those using traditional biomass, we have around 1.3 billion who need help to have access to alternative energy.

If we think of the supply chain distribution of energy during market volatility and supply disruptions, renewable energy will be a solution. Of course, the major contributions of RE to sustainable development are its environmental and health benefits.

Bioluminescent Light: A Green Energy Solution

There is another Green Energy solution to the search for other environment-friendly sources of energy. From the frontiers of science, particularly from synthetic biology, there is an emerging Green Energy solution which we call bioluminescent light. This is the topic of this book. We are providing you with more details about this green energy innovation in later chapters.

The phenomenon of bioluminescence as a possible source of energy is still emerging. This kind of energy does not have carbon footprint, so it has a good potential as an environment-friendly source of light. It mimics the light being produced by some creatures from land and sea such as the light of the fireflies, squid, jellyfish, glowworms, and the algae. When we try to mimic nature, we call it biomimicry.

Bioluminescent light is an untapped energy which is still poorly understood by many. It is considered a disruptive innovation of the future. At this time, there is still no commercialized product using bioluminescent lighting system in the market. It does not produce heat since the energy comes from a biological source that emits cold light. It cannot fully replace electricity as a source of light but it can last longer or even perpetually for as long as the host that produces the light is still alive.

PART TWO

The Dream and the Imagination

CHAPTER 4

The Dream: Light from Fireflies

As we were writing this book, we always would go back to that moment when we realized that we both shared the same dream and experience of being fascinated with the light of the fireflies when we were children. The amazing part is that we were born from two different countries of Southeast Asia. We were born in the same situation in a small village but in separate countries: one from the Philippines and the other from Thailand. We both encountered the light from the fireflies and were fascinated by this light. In those times when there was no electricity, the light of the fireflies was a welcome sight. It lighted our way.

Both during our childhood days, as we were growing up in two different countries in villages where electricity was not available, we were fascinated by the light of the fireflies. In our child's mind, we had many questions:

Why does a firefly have light?

What is the purpose of the light of the firefly?

How does a firefly produce light?

Can we mimic this light produced by the firefly?

Is it only the firefly that produces its own light?

As children, we had this natural curiosity about the wonders of nature and we asked many candid questions. Such is the nature of children. We never forgot the experience of fireflies as we grew up, not aware of each other since we were living in different countries and had not yet met each other at that time.

Let us share with you our shared dream of inventing living light inspired by fireflies, a dream that began during our childhood days.

Thirteen years ago, we met each other in the Philippines in the university where both of us were working in different fields. We would share a lot of our experiences in the different countries where we came from, and then we realized that we both had very similar experiences when it came to fireflies. Each living in a village without the light coming from electricity, we saw darkness during the night and yet hundreds of fireflies would also light our way in that darkness. Thus began our commitment for the realization of a shared dream. We did not know the way, but we were certain that there was a way and that the universe would eventually conspire to let us achieve what we desired.

Those were amazing discussions we had, having the same passion and interest in how the fireflies produce light and we promised that one day, when we would have more knowledge,we would create a light similar to the light of the firefly. It was an elusive dream back then. We both continued with our lives, myself in the Philippines, and he in Thailand first and then in the United States where he involved himself for quite some time in his business. We then lived separate lives.

Today, after thirteen years, we met again in the Philippines. We returned to our shared dream on how we could invent together a lighting system that would make use of bioluminescence. We still had the desire to understand deeply the phenomenon of bioluminescence, and so we agreed on a plan to earn more knowledge, to engage in research and start up the bioluminescent perpetual light.

It was reassuring that both of us were working in the same direction and that we complement each other in this scientific project. We had the same passion, tenacity, and drive to achieve a seemingly impossible invention. We both believed in our BIG dream. We were thinking big, but we could only act small. That we fiercely believed in our BIG dream – could this be just another strategy?

We also started to look for venture capitalists who would be willing to invest on our startup project. Who would believe us despite the fact that they still had not seen a prototype? We were taking small steps to reach our BIG dream.

An imagined street lighted by the GlowGlobe perpetual bioluminescent lamps.

CHAPTER 5

The Importance of Imagination

The most quoted adage of Albert Einstein is about how much he valued imagination more than knowledge. When he said, "Imagination is more important than knowledge," he is referring to the unique human capacity to envision that which is not there and which belongs to the future. If we have great imagination, we can think of ideas that defy existing knowledge. That is why inventors and innovators are a rare breed of individuals who think of ideas never before imagined or envisioned. The gift of imagination enables the individual to see many alternative futures and choose that future which will preserve the human civilization.

World-famous author J.K. Rowling (2008) likewise believes in the crucial importance of imagination. She has learned to value imagination not only because it enabled her to create the magical Harry Potter world, but because imagination is the "fount of inventions and innovations." She also believes that imagination is the power that "enables us to emphatize with humans whose experiences we have never shared." (Rowling, 2008).

In this book, we talk of imagination as the prime mover of innovative ideas as well as disruptive innovations. Without the power of our imagination, we would never have been able to imagine an alternative lighting system that depends not on electricity but on a biological source of light. Imagination enables us to examine different worlds, much like Einstein who imagined thirty different worlds before he finally came to a deep understanding of the general theory of relativity. This human ability to imagine is what differentiates us from animals and the lower life forms as well as from artificial intelligence and machine learning. In this imagined world, new discoveries are made and new inventions are created. How had we imagined a future where bioluminescent light is an alternative source of light?

This is the story. We were both fascinated with the ability of fireflies to glow in the dark, to emit their own light from their bodies. This is natural light and we somehow sensed that something in their genetic make up is enabling them to produce the light naturally. This is the beauty of the natural world. According to Vierra (2011), for billions of years, nature – animals, plants, and even microbes – has been solving many of the problems that the world still face today.

Benyus (1997) believes that most of the problems that have ever existed have already been solved by nature. She suggests that instead of us learning about nature, we should be learning from nature. She terms this experience as biomimicry. So, we asked ourselves: why don't we mimic the light of the firefly? Why not invent a product that is fueled by a biological source of light, much like the firefly which takes for granted that it is able to produce light so as to attract a mate?

Imagination enables us to see the world in a grain of sand and eternity in a flower. Imagination enabled us to see bioluminescence as an alternative green energy. We imagined a world where street lamps are fueled by bioluminescence, suspended in the air, without the usual lamp posts since these street lamps are not dependent on electricity. They light up avenues at less costs. Malls and buildings, as well as subdivisions, are using the bioluminescent lighting systems. The 1.4 billion people in the world who are in the dark because electricity is non-existent for them might as well be enjoying bioluminescent light. The problem of darkness is thus eliminated.

But imagination alone could not have brought us to this point where we are already about to embark on the production of the prototype. We also need passion, that intense desire to achieve what we want, and to pursue it relentlessly. Passion is what wakes us up in the morning, eager to look for possibilities to explore solutions to the challenge posed to us by prototyping. Passion is an inner drive that propels us to be innovative, to continue to seek solutions despite facing setbacks along the way.

Passion, perseverance, infinite patience, creativity and innovation – these are the hallmarks that have guided us in our search for ways to make our BIG dream become a reality. We began the search for the venture capital by which to finance the big cost entailed in coming up with a molecular biology laboratory to produce the prototype. We first did our pitch to the Philippine Venture Capital Investment Group (Philvencap), the biggest group of venture capitalists, investors, and entrepreneurs in the Philippines. There were some investors interested in our project.

That was also the time when we joined the pitching competition of IDE (Innovation-Driven Entrepreneurship) in October of 2017. We were officially admitted in November 2017 to the IDE Accelerator 2018 Program of Thailand and MIT in Boston, Massachusetts. The idea was that we would undergo training and coaching until we were able to perfect our product idea. We were called the Team Perpetual Light Biotechnologies. While polishing our product idea, we were also looking for the best way to create a prototype. We were not able to proceed to the competition proper because we were not able to deliver our prototype on time.

What now? Our long–term plan is to search for universities overseas which will be willing to offer us a scholarship for a PhD with our project as our proposal.

Meanwhile, we decided to write this book, so readers worldwide will not have to give up early on in their dream.

CHAPTER 6

Biomimicry:
Mimicking the Firefly

There is a very interesting field of study, being promoted by Janine Benyus, an advocate of the idea of us, humans, learning from nature. It is called Biomimicry which Benyus popularized in her 1997 book, *Biomimicry: Innovation Inspired by Nature*. We resonate with her philosophy and her passion and we recognize that our product idea of bioluminescent light belongs to Biomimicry. Our lighting system which we call GlowGlobe is a disruptive innovation inspired by nature, in particular by a firefly. Thus, we believe that we should take up her cause – to make the world aware of how we can learn so much by learning how nature has survived for billions of years.

Benyus (1997) defines biomimicry as "the science and

art of emulating Nature's best biological ideas to solve human problems." For instance, our dream was to offer an alternative solution to the use of electricity, without depositing carbon footprint. So, we looked at nature and we found out that nature could provide a solution. Our fascination with fireflies and other bioluminescent creatures in sea and on land led us to bio-energy, to learning how fireflies produce natural light. Can we mimic the light of the firefly? How can the fireflies teach us what they do so naturally without having to bother about fossil fuels?

Indeed, the biological world offers us possible solutions to the world's pressing problems. There are many examples of innovative designs with which we are familiar, all inspired by nature. Take, for instance, Leonardo da Vinci who applied biomimicry when designing human flight. He made many sketches of birds in flight in his lifetime, trying to unlock the secrets of why birds could fly. Although he was never able to invent the airplane, yet his observations inspired the Wright Brothers to study the pigeons and seek to know what enabled them to fly in the sky. The Wright Brothers finally succeeded in 1903 to design what we now know as airplane. This is the ultimate exemplar of biomimicry. Other inventors and innovators followed suit, realizing that by learning from nature, they could find solutions to some of today's pressing needs.

Benyus (1997), quoting Vaclav Havel, President of the Czech Republic, said, "We must draw our standards from the natural world. We must honor with the humility of the wise the bounds of the natural world and the mystery which lies beyond them, admitting that there is something in the order of being which evidently exceeds all our competence." Her point is that we should go back and learn from nature and its standards in order to design innovative products. The standards of the natural world have survived 4.2 billion of years of existence on Earth. Nature-inspired innovations should be in the service of the Earth, and not to destroy it. There is very real possibility that in the next 30 years we will lose a quarter of all the Earth's species by the humans' wanton disregard of the natural safeguards. Biomimicry will then be not just a way of looking at nature, but "a race and a rescue." (Benyus, 1997).

Biomimicry: Mimicking the Light of Fireflies

What is valuable about the Biomimicry Movement is that it provides us with a tool called Biomimicry Design Spiral that uses nature as a model. We would like to apply this model or framework to the phenomenon of light production of the fireflies. The steps are as follows:

Identify. *Develop a Design Brief of the human need.* In this first step, we identified the need for green energy that will reduce carbon footprint and protect the environment, in general. We developed the need for an alternative lighting system for the future.

Interpret. *Biologize the question by asking the design brief from Nature's perspective.* Ask, "How does Nature do this function?" "How does Nature NOT do this function?" Guided by these biological questions, we asked ourselves the

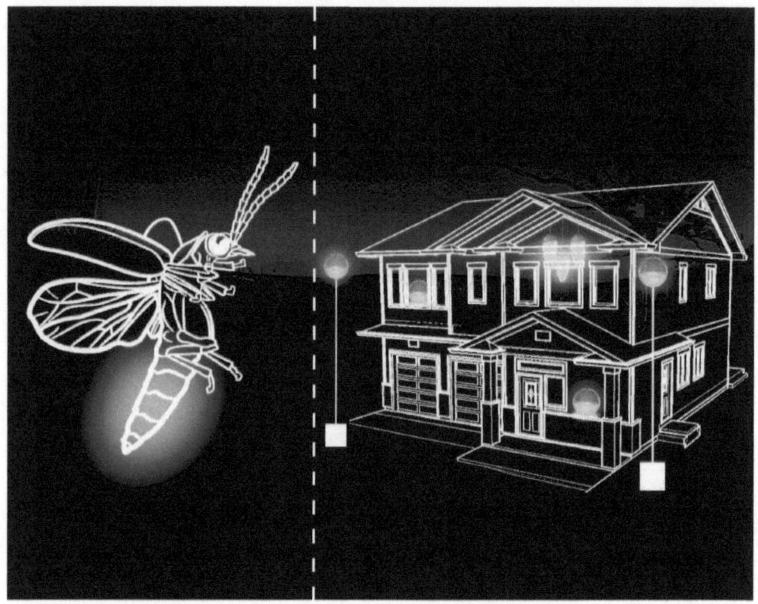

A sketch of the light of a firefly being mimicked as a source of living light for a home.

question, "How does the firefly do this function of producing light? Why do other creatures do not do this function? Why is it that only some species like firefly, squid and jelly fish, among others, are able to have bioluminescence?

Discover. *Look for the champions in nature which can answer/resolve your challenges.* Here, in the discovery part, we considered other creatures in the natural world, like in the oceans and seas, and on land. For example, we discovered, when we did intensive research, many other bioluminescent sea creatures, such as squid, jelly fish, sea urchins, some types of fish, algaes, and glowworms.

Abstract. *Find the repeating patterns and processes*

within nature that achieve success. Bioluminescent creatures are abundant in nature. They use their bioluminescent light for protection, to ward off prey, to attract mates, or to find their way into the deep, dark ocean. The patterns and processes can be studied. That is our goal, our BIG project. To understand the secrets of bioluminescent fireflies.

Emulate. *Develop ideas and design solutions based on the natural models.* Then we developed the idea of mimicking how the fireflies produce their light in their bodies. We looked for solutions from the natural world and from science and technology, and we adopted biotechnology and synthetic biology as our processes to come up with perpetual bioluminescent light for the use of humans.

Evaluate. *How do ideas compare with the successful principles of nature?* In this step, we compared the processes of synthetic biology to that of the successful principles of nature. We realized that it could be done. By genetically modifying the genes of microbes to create the chemical reaction needed to produce the living light, we could produce our perpetual lighting system using the concept of bioluminescence.

Identify. *In the process of being iterative, develop and refine the design briefs based on the lessons learned from the evaluation of Life's Principles.* Looking at our project proposal which we submitted to the IDE coaches, we need to refine our design brief and see to it that the microorganism as host should be non-toxic and non-pathogenic. In the natural world, nothing is toxic or pathogenic because it is the nature of the creatures to produce the bioluminescent light. But once we use synthetic biology and re-engineeer the genes of the host to be used for the lighting system of humans, we need to be cautious and evaluate the extent of risks that we may unwittingly create as we produce our prototype.

An imagined room being lighted by the GlowGlobe perpetual bioluminescent lighting system as lamps and a bio light panel.

CHAPTER 7

Breakthrough with Bioluminescence

What is wonderful about science is that it is responsible for our modern progress. Without science and the many scientists who devoted their entire lifetime to the pursuit of new discoveries, breakthroughs, and new frontiers, we would never have advanced to a point where artificial intelligence could do for us our mundane and repetitive tasks.

For many years, we have heard of scientific inventions and how these have contributed to the advancement of science and technology. The Industry 4.0 has brought about many technological innovations in biotechnology, artificial intelligence, nanotechnology, synthetic biology, and space exploration. We admire the innovators who dared to dream and pursued their dream until they made a breakthrough, from the cloud of unknowing to a bright sunshine and silver lining where the darkness vanished. Most of them have won a Nobel Prize in science. They are our heroes, our mentors, our sources of inspiration. We would like to follow their path toward scientific discovery.

When we talk of breakthroughs in science and technology, we mean those discoveries that have penetrated the cloud of unknowing and brought us into a bright, new world. Technological breakthroughs enable us to enjoy many new technologically-driven products and services, as well as make our life comfortable, among others. We owe much to the inventors and innovators who made all this possible for us.

It took quite a while for us to experience a breakthrough with our product idea. We needed to understand many things about the invention. So, we did what any researchers would do: we did intensive research. We learned a lot from our investigative research; we learned about gene cells and gene splicing, we learned how to set up a molecular biology laboratory, and we learned about synthetic biology.

In the course of our research, we realized that there were pioneers in the bioluminescent light potential for alternative energy. We were not alone; there were others ahead of us in the path we were traversing. They tried to look into the potential of the phenomenon of bioluminescence as a source of light for humanity in a different way, but all of them had been inspired by the bioluminescent organisms. Their outputs were similar, such as the following:

TAXA Biotechnologies located in the USA was also

inspired by the light of the firefly to generate bioluminescent light. We researched and watched their video on how they did a pitch for crowd funding about their glowing trees product idea before a big crowd. The commonality is in the term "glow". We are all mesmerized by the "glowing" ability of bioluminescent creatures, e.g. to glow in the dark. The TAXA Biotechnologies business idea goes like this: They were envisioning bioluminescent trees providing light along streets and avenues. Plant these glowing trees on both sides of an avenue and there will be no need to use street lamps fueled by electricity. Five years ago, it was such a great idea and it held so much promise. Imagine a world where we have glowing trees and plants replacing our lampshades, our street lights, and, in general, our lighting systems.

We know that we need to learn from their experience and derive from them important insights to develop our own invention of bioluminescent perpetual light product. We would like to thank their company that gives us the inspiration for our project and for taking the lead in Asia and the world and focusing on the 1400 million persons still in darkness.

We also learned about the Glowee Company in France. We are proud of their attempt to develop a lighting system using bioluminescence inspired by the squid. Again, we share a similar fascination for the term "glow". They were able to produce the prototype, and sell some of their lighting systems to the malls. They are finding ways to extend the duration of their bioluminescent light. This also provides inspiration for us to create a bioluminescent perpetual lighting system as a leader in Asia and the world.

The last pioneer that we got to know through our research is a professor of chemical engineering at the Massachusetts Institute of Technology (MIT). He was successful in producing a glowing watercress plant. He and his MIT team packaged each of these components into a different type of nanoparticle carrier. The nanoparticles helped them to get to the right part of the plant and also prevented them from building to concentrations that could be toxic to the plants. The result was a watercress plant that functioned like a desk lamp which they called Celestine alluding to the Celestial light.

These, then, are the pioneers in bioluminescent light potential who came before us and inspired us to engage in disruptive innovation. We differentiate the GlowGlobe product idea by envisioning a perpetual lighting system fueled by bioluminescence. We have an ambitious goal of coming up with a perpetual lighting system with bioluminescence. We are likewise inspired by the light of the firefly and we are attempting to mimic this living light with our own idea of applying synthetic biology as our process of genetically modifying friendly microorganisms that will serve as hosts that produce the bioluminescent light in our lighting product.

What is distinct about our project lies in the process of producing the perpetual bioluminescent lighting system.

In other words, we were able to finally make a breakthrough after a rigorous process of researching into what we needed to know to produce our prototype the way we envisioned it, a unique invention that aims to produce a perpetual lighting system that uses bioluminescence. And we made this breakthrough by way of an obscure paper written 68 years ago!

PART THREE

On the Phenomenon of Bioluminescence

CHAPTER 8

Bioluminescence 101: The Basics

The phenomenon of bioluminescence is the focus of this book and it is our aim to provide a general understanding of bioluminescence in order to raise the readers' awareness for this fascinating topic which is a part of the wonders of the natural world.

What is bioluminescence?

Bioluminescence is defined as a light produced by a chemical reaction within a living organism. Hence, we call it living light as opposed to artificial light like the electric light that we are familiar with. While electricity as a source of light emits thermal heat, bioluminescent light emits what is called "cold light". This means that the light produced by bioluminescent organisms is comprised only of 20% of thermal radiation or heat. We cannot expect bioluminescent light to take over the use of electricity but it can significantly reduce our electricity costs. Likewise, bioluminescence is a type of chemiluminescence, meaning, there is a chemical reaction happening within the living organism that produces light. If we can unravel the secret of how this chemical reaction occurs, and what causes it, what are the chemicals involved, we can begin to understand how this natural light can be put to good use for humans.

The chemical energy in bioluminescent organisms is what we would like to understand as it is released as natural light in the natural environment. For billions of years, these bioluminescent organisms have been emitting light and have survived by making use of their ability to produce light, be it by warding off preys in the deep ocean, or by attracting mate for the survival of the species, or by attacking other sea creatures for food; they have been doing it as a matter of course, no big deal. Yet, for us humans, this is a big deal because of our urgent need for alternative sources of energy. Here is a biological source of light that can be a potential source of energy for humanity and yet so far, it has not yet been commercialized.

According to Branchini (2004), bioluminescence "is an enchanting process in which living organisms convert chemical energy into light." He further pointed out that in nature, there is an amazing diversity of organisms that emit light such as bacteria, fungi, crustaceans, mollusks, fishes, and insects (Hastings, 1995, cited in Branchini, 2004). They are in oceans but also on land such as fireflies and snails; they inhabit the natural world. Those who have been down the deep ocean have surely encountered these bioluminescent sea creatures which have provided them, human creatures, with the light whereby to see while swimming on the ocean floor. The algaes, the glowworms, the squids, the mollusks, and the fishes, all in one way or the other emit bioluminescent light, with varying colors.

Strangely enough, there are no bioluminescent organisms found in fresh water environment like lakes and ponds. It would be interesting to know why. Some reasons provided are that firstly, fresh water habitats have not been around as long as marine habitats have, so their evolution is slow unlike in the oceans, not enough biodiversity that has evolved here for billions of years. And secondly, the fresh water organisms do not really need bioluminescence to survive.

Types of Bioluminescent Light

Let us talk about the varying colors of the bioluminescent light of these light-producing organisms. It is usual for marine bioluminescent organisms like squid, fishes, jellyfish, mollusks, and sea cucumber, among others, to exhibit blue to green colored light based on the visible light spectrum of light. A good explanation can be that this makes it easier for these sea creatures to navigate the deep ocean while also camouflaging them from unwanted preys. The habitat where they are found could likewise be responsible for this phenomenon.

For instance, if when found in oceans, the marine organisms produce blue-green light. Their genetic make up dictates the kind of color their light will be. It is interesting to note that they cannot produce colors like yellow, red, or violet due perhaps to the chemistry of their bioluminescence, which means that the kind of chemical reaction that is happening in their bodies that is responsible for the color they emit. Because of this ability to emit colored light, the first use of bioluminescent light was as a gene promoter which won for its inventors a Nobel Prize in 2008. Because of this invention, medical doctors can now trace the color of the gene promoter, by which to detect certain diseases or illnesses inside a human body. They use it as in vivo imaging to visualize tumors and to monitor gene expression and regulation (Branchini, 2010). We will know more about this in Chapter 9 when we discuss the chemistry of firefly bioluminescence.

Now, as to terrestrial bioluminescent organisms such as insects like fireflies or beetles, algaes on land, and the only snail that produces bioluminescent light, the *Quantula striata* which is found in the tropics of Southeast Asia, all these organisms produce yellow color. Although some likewise produce blue to green light. But the most common color they emit is the yellow of the color spectrum. Thus, if we mimic the fireflies, we expect yellow light for our perpetual lighting system. The land which is their habitat may be also responsible for their yellow color.

However, since synthetic biology can alter the colors produced by bioluminescent organisms so we need not stick to just the yellow color in the near future. We will see this possibility in Chapter 17 of this book. Suffice to say that, not only is bioluminescent light a rare phenomenon in nature but it is also colorful in the sense that we get to watch varying colors as we study different organisms on land and in seas. The biological source of light is an amazing natural phenomenon and the possibilities for its being used in the service of humanity are staggering.

Historical Background of Bioluminescence

Even in ancient times, the phenomenon of bioluminescence was already recognized although not in as scientific a way as we do today. Hunters in those times used the light of the fireflies as they went hunting in the forests. In the 1880s Pliny the Elder used the bioluminescent light of the squid for his adventures. Even Charles Darwin (1859) aboard his Beagle already noticed the bioluminescent marine organisms and wondered about them.

Thérèse Wilson and Woody Hastings (2013) explored the natural history, evolution, and biochemistry of the diverse array of organisms that emit light in their book, *Living Lights, Lights for the Living* (Wilson and Hastings, 2013). The authors wrote the book because they believed that while there were already several available books concerned with some specific aspects and scientific details of bioluminescence, there were none that explored both the diversity of biochemical reactions and the similarity of their chemical mechanisms, while covering the entire field.

They pointed out that while some bacteria, mushrooms, and invertebrates, as well as fish, are bioluminescent, other vertebrates and plants are not. There are no bioluminescent plants at all. Thus, the attempts to produce glowing trees and plants using bioluminescence are met with skepticism. But, history can tell that those that were dubbed "crazy ideas" proved to be inventions that changed our lives and moved the wheels of progress and modernity.

Furthermore, Wilson and Hastings (2013) noted that the sporadic distribution and paucity of luminous forms calls for explanation, as does the fact that unrelated groups have evolved completely different biochemical pathways to luminescence. The authors explore the hypothesis that many different luciferase systems arose in the early evolution of life because of their ability to remove oxygen, which was toxic to life when it first appeared on earth.

They remarked that as oxygen became abundant and bioluminescence was no longer adequate for oxygen removal, other antioxidant mechanisms evolved and most luminous species became extinct. This is how bioluminescence evolved through time.

An earlier book of E. Newton Harvey, *A History of Luminescence From the Earliest Times Until 1900* which was published in 1957 in Philadelphia by The American Philosophical Society (Volume 44 of the Memoirs) likewise looked into the historical evolution of the phenomenon of bioluminescence from the earliest time until 1900. This is a good source of reference when we would like to trace the beginning of this topic on bioluminescence.

A History of Marine Bioluminescence

In 1957, E. Newton Harvey published a book, *A History of Luminescence* (Harvey, 1957) where he came up with an annotated history of marine bioluminescence. He died in 1959. During his lifetime, he was dubbed, "Dean of Bioluminescence" since he devoted his whole life on this research area. His annotated history which spans from 500 BC to 1774. In this annotated history, Harvey gives the dates, the names of the authors/famous personalities or scientists, and their findings regarding the phenomenon of marine bioluminescence. This is an amazing annotation, to say the least, a wonderful research of a lifetime.

We will start from 500 B.C. to 215 B.C. There were three observations in 500 B.C., 350 B.C. and 215 B.C., by Anaximenes, Aristotle, and Titus Livius, all ancient philosophers. All three described bioluminescence in the sea as "light", "lightning" and "fire". Quoting Livius, he related luminescence to fire – "the sea was aflame" and "the shores (were) luminous with frequent fires."

In 50 A.D., Pliny the Elder made his famous remark describing the luminous slime of *"Pulmo marinus"* (jellyfish) as follows: "a walking stick rubbed with the pulmo marinus will light the way like a torch" He also mentioned the luminescence of glowworms, the mollusc Pholas, and the lantern fish *"Lucerna pieces"*. His observations contributed a lot to our knowledge of bioluminescence.

From 1605 to 1774, there were also many observations made about the living light coming from the marine organisms that were included in Harvey's seminal book. From Francis Bacon, Rene Descartes, Robert Boyle to Sir Issac Newton and Benjamin Franklin are among the famous personalities in the world who shared their experience about the bioluminescent marine species, thus increasing significantly our understanding of them.

CHAPTER 9

How Does A Firefly Create Bioluminescence?

Our main concern in the development of bioluminescence lighting technology is how to mimic the living light of fireflies. Hence, we need to understand the chemistry of firefly bioluminescence.

The Nature of Fireflies

Our main interest is focused on the firefly and not on other species that emit light. We know them as fireflies but the truth is that they belong to the family of beetles whose scientific name is *Lampyridae*. For some scientists, these are better known as lightning bugs. For our purpose, however, we will call them simply as fireflies. It is surprising to know that there are 2,000 species of beetles worldwide and they live in different environments or habitats, each behaving differently from one another. There are some beetles that do not glow at all. As for those that emit light, we can usually find the light producing organ of adult fireflies on the lower parts of their abdomens.

The pioneering work on firefly bioluminescence of William McElroy, Emil White, and Howard Seliger in 1957 provides us with enough information to understand how fireflies produce light. Their basic research focused on the North American firefly called *Photinus pyralis*. Through their research, they were able to understand how fireflies produce light.

Among the most complex adaptations of bioluminescence to be found in nature are those exhibited by fireflies, which are also among the most intensely studied luminescent organisms (McElroy, 1950). From the male firefly's point of view, mating is a task that cannot be taken lightly (meaning, it should be taken seriously. This is for the survival of their species.) He must fly about at the proper altitude and at the proper speed, at the proper time of the evening during the proper time of the year, and emit light in the appropriate manner, merely to succeed in attracting the attention of a female of his own species. He must then continue flashing his light and approaching her in a correct way, or she will stop responding to him and he will lose her. Such are the ways of courtships among the fireflies and the bioluminescent light is thus crucial to this mating behavior between male and female fireflies.

Further in the region extending east and southwest

from India to the Philippines and New Guinea, fireflies have evolved patterns of flashing behavior far different from that of the North American fireflies. In areas stretching for miles along the rivers and swamps of Asia and the Pacific Islands, several species of fireflies gather in trees each night, swarming by the thousands. The insects take time out from their flashing duties only to mate.

The Bioluminescence Process

The wonder of bioluminescence is that this is the process of converting chemical energy into light. According to Branchini (2010), what is happening in this chemical process is that there is what is described as the oxidation "of an organic substrate, a luciferin, catalyzed by an enzyme called a luciferase." The chemical reaction results in the production of light, a process which appears so simple and so natural for these organisms. No light will be emitted if there is no interaction between an enzyme-mediated reaction between molecular oxygen and organic substrate. This is the minimum condition for the creation of bioluminescent light. Another thing that was pointed out by Branchini (2010) is that there is the possibility of the breaking down of a four-member ring peroxide or a linear hydroperoxide (Wilson, 1995, Wood, 1995, cited in Branchini, 2010).

What are the Biochemical Reactions
of Firefly Bioluminescence?

For the biochemical reactions of firefly bioluminescence,

we need the expert guide of scientists. Everything looks very complicated when we go into the complexities of chemical bonding and oxidation but nature is never actually complicated because parsimony is its goal.

For the uninitiated, the biochemical process is complex and daunting but yet we are only looking at the chemicals luciferin, luciferase, and ATP or the adenosine triphosphate as the universal biochemical energy source.

Bioluminescent reaction occurs when organic molecules known generally as luciferins are oxidized in the presence of enzymes called luciferases. In this process, luciferin is converted through the process of oxidation from low energy ground state compound to one of high energy, or "excited" state. It then loses its energy by radiating a photon of visible light, yielding an oxidized form of luciferin as a by-product. Light is generated until all luciferin has been oxidized. The reaction is remarkably efficient with virtually no energy wasted as heat – hence the term "cold light." (McElroy, 1950).

In the 1947 paper of McElroy, titled *"The Energy Source for Bioluminescence in an Isolated System"*, he reported his observation that adding adenosine triphosphate (ATP), a high-energy compound found in all living cells, to samples of ground fireflies caused a brilliant flash of light to appear immediately, which persisted for considerable time, depending upon the concentration of the ATP. (Note: Ground fireflies means that the light-emitting organ of fireflies called lanterns were dried and grounded to powder form). Because of this discovery of McElroy, it has been found that ATP functions with luciferase in catalyzing the reaction between luciferin and molecular oxygen in firefly bioluminescence.

Every application of bioluminescence in industry and in laboratory derives its usefulness from the fact that ATP and FMNH2 (flavin mono-nucleotide – a compound highly important in cellular respiration – and a long chain aldehyde) are the limiting factors for the amount and intensity of light radiated from a sample. This is an important result of McElroy's experiment, that we are able to identify the limiting factor for the amount and intensity of bioluminescent light. If we can harness this knowledge in our search for the best solution to our product idea, we will be able to bring the bioluminescent light to streets and homes throughout the world. Such is our goal as researchers and inventors.

In the case of firefly bioluminescence, preparations of the purified luciferin or luciferase, or crude extracts of the firefly's light-generating organs or lanterns – and even the dried lanterns themselves – can be used to test for the presence of ATP and for monitoring ATP converting reaction (i.e. this is crude by 2018 standards; we now have synthetic biology and biotechnology, instead).

McElroy (1950) was one of the pioneer researchers on bioluminescence. He pointed out that the production of light in firefly extracts depends upon a heat-bubble catalyst (luciferase), a heat-stable yellow-green fluorescent compound (luciferin an inorganic ion), oxygen, and ATP. The necessity of phosphate bond energy for light production suggests the existence of an energy- coupling reaction between ATP and some component of the luminescent system, presumably the luciferin-luciferase complex.

Finally, on the utilization of ATP in a luminescent system, one of the interesting characteristics of the luminescent system was the rapidity with which ATP was apparently utilized. The findings from this experiment is that it is ATP that is the limiting factor for firefly bioluminescence. When more ATP is added to the preparations, then the light becomes brighter and the duration longer.

CHAPTER 10

Firefly Bioluminescence: Perspective from an Entomologist from Thailand

Rationale of the Interview

On April 4, 2018, Dr. Soontorn Piromsartkoon, one of the authors of this book, conducted an interview in Bangkok with Assistant Professor, Dr. Anchana Thancharoen of the Department of Entomology, Faculty of Agriculture, Kasetsart University, Bangkok, Thailand. Dr. Anchana is an entomologist who has devoted 16 years of her life in the study of fireflies and their conservation.

We wanted to know her opinions, comments, and experiences with fireflies, and get advice from her regarding firefly bioluminescence, our perpetual bioluminescent lighting system, and the future of sustainability and survival of the fireflies. The interview yielded interesting findings.

About the Entomologist

The Entomologist that Dr. Soontorn Piromsartkoon interviewed is Dr. Anchana Thancharoen of the Department of Entomology, Faculty of Agriculture of the University of Kasetsart University in Bangkok, Thailand. She holds a PhD Biology from Mahidol University in Bangkok in 2007. Her dissertation on fireflies is titled, "Biology and Mating Behavior of an Aquatic Firefly Species, *Luciola aquatilis Thancharoen*" which is presently renamed as *Sclerotia aquatilis*. For her master's degree, she finished an M.S. in Environmental Biology in 2001, with her thesis, "Study on Diversity of Firefly Populations in Highland and Lowland Habitats." Her research interests are mostly on the study of the fireflies' mating behavior, sexual selection, and sexual communication, as well as research topics on Ecology Conservation and Cassava pests. She has spent 16 years of her life on the study of fireflies and has published a total of 10 scholarly articles on the topic. Most importantly, Dr. Anchana has published a book written in the Thai language, *The Common of an Uncommon Insect 'Firefly'* (Thancharoen, 2009). There is a need for this little book with colorful photographs of the firefly communities to be translated into English, so it could reach the English-speaking readers in the world.

On the 16 Years of Study of Fireflies

Dr. Anchana has devoted 16 years of her life to the study of fireflies. We might wonder why someone would devote long years of study on just one insect. But that is how

Close up photo of a firefly in the Firefly Learning Center, Kasetsart University, Bangkok, Thailand. Photo courtesy of Dr. Anchana Thanchareon, April 4, 2018, Bangkok, Thailand.

---

scientists are. They are so focused and busy researching that they forget that the years have passed by. But in the process of this devotion to a lifetime work, they are able to contribute greatly to the advancement of science. They are the unsung heroes of our time.

We wanted to know the reasons why Dr. Anchana devoted her life on firefly and what motivated her for this lifetime study.

Acknowledging that Dr. Achana has made a great contribution to the advancement on the understanding of the nature of fireflies, we asked her how she got interested in the study of fireflies and became an entomologist. She said that she had a childhood fascination with fireflies. Likewise, she had a beautiful experience with them that inspired her to go into deeper study of the fireflies and how to protect them for their sustainability as creatures of living light.

Based on her long years of research on the fireflies in Thailand, Dr. Anchana noted that the sustainability of fireflies as bioluminescent organisms is being threatened by light pollution as well as chemical pollution, destruction of their natural habitat, global climate change, and other environmental threats to their existence. There is an urgent need, she pointed out, to provide sanctuaries to create their natural environment. In their university, they established a Firefly Learning Center where the fireflies are in their natural environment; here deeper studies on their behavior like

A firefly field with swarms of fireflies during evening. Photo courtesy by Dr. Anchana Thancharoen, April 4, 2018, Bangkok, Thailand.

flashing behavior, mating behavior, and rearing behavior are being conducted by students and researchers.

We also wanted to know the evolutionary origins of fireflies as bioluminescent organism as well as get her insights that Dr. Anchana on the survival of the bioluminescent fireflies over the long term.

According to Dr. Anchana, the firefly's evolution has a long history. She has devoted 16 years of study on their natural characteristics, their behavior through time, their means of survival, their habitat, their mating time, and their breeding time. In short, she said, she has done an in-depth and longitudinal study that enabled her to have a deeper understanding of this type of beetle and their role in the natural environment.

Today, with the environment so polluted, the fireflies are slowly disappearing. Pollution affects not only the fireflies but also the humans. In agriculture, the presence of fireflies is a part of the symbiosis and, if fireflies will go extinct as a species, then we will lose one creature of living light. One type of firefly that Dr. Anchana is studying is a mangrove species which is a natural enemy of fresh water snails. There is a need to protect these fireflies and provide them, if possible, with the sanctuaries where they can live in a natural environment that will ensure their survival over the long term.

On Bioluminescence Technology

We informed Dr. Anchana that we were writing this book and we wanted to know her opinions and perspective as an entomologist on the phenomenon of bioluminescence as an alternative source of light for humans. We told her that we were using biotechnology and synthetic biology to come up with products using bioluminescence inspired by the light of the fireflies.

She said that she had heard of it before but apologized that this might not be within her expertise nor within her field of study. She was interested in the protection of fireflies for their long term survival. However, she believed that the book we were writing could have a significant impact on how the world would look at the fireflies as creatures of living light.

She also believed that what we were doing on the light being emitted by fireflies was an interesting development. She said she would be happy to learn more about this innovation and the process of producing the bioluminescent light of fireflies using synthetic biology.

We inquired about the prospects that she could foresee for those like us who were developing lighting systems using bioluminescence as the source of light and we asked her opinion about the developments in biotechnology and synthetic biology, such as in producing glowing trees or lighting systems as a form of green energy.

Interestingly, Dr. Anchana remarked that the first to commercialize the bioluminescent light would be making a breakthrough and would thus be a pioneering spirit. She expressed her happiness that the bioluminescent light emitted by fireflies could be mimicked and then harnessed as green energy for humans. As to the possibility of glowing trees as bioluminescent light, she expressed her concern that this might affect the ecological ecosystem. She pointed out, among others, these concerns: 1.) the relationships between plants and pests; 2.) deterrence against natural enemies; and 3.) effect on the food chain and food web.

With regards to glowing trees, she understood that these were genetically modified trees. She expressed concern that there might be some effects on the ecosystem.

By way of conclusion, she remarked that if our perpetual bioluminescent lighting system would become commercially viable, then we would be making a great contribution to science and industry.

Bioluminescent Lighting System as Disruptive innovation

Since we envisioned bioluminescent lighting system as a disruptive innovation of the future, we asked Dr. Anchana what she thought would be the cost implications of such a development and how its benefits could be assured to outweigh its cost of production. She responded that she thought that it would be costly at the start; however, if we could have venture capital funding this would help lessen the startup costs. She added that the setting up of a molecular biology laboratory would be very expensive; the sourcing out of friendly microbes as hosts of the bioluminescent light would be among the cost considerations. There would also be a need to hire experts and scientists to implement the invention, and such persons could be difficult to find. Moreover, expenses related to patents and securing

The book of Dr. Anchana Tancharoen in Thai language version, titled, **The Common of an Uncommon Insect "firefly."** (Thancharoen, 2009).

government requirements for operating a laboratory and engaging in biotechnology, more so, synthetic biology, would entail a lot of initial investments.

We informed her that we were among the few technology innovators intending to come up with a lighting system using bioluminescence inspired by the light of the fireflies. We asked Dr. Anchana what she thought would be our chances of succeeding with this invention.

She told us that we needed scientists and experts on biotechnology and synthetic biology as members of our team. She was sure it would take some time for us to succeed; we would need enough trials in the laboratory, first to produce the prototype as a proof that our product idea would work. If we would succeed, she said, our perpetual bioluminescent lighting product would be the first product to be commercialized using bioluminescence as a source of light. However, she said, our great challenge would be precisely that this might be difficult to achieve.

The Future of Fireflies

We asked her as a seasoned expert on fireflies what would be the future of these creators of light in the natural world in the face of pollution and global climate change? What steps could we take to ensure the long term survival of our bioluminescent organisms like fireflies, glowworms, and algae? What would be her role in protecting these creatures of living light which were illuminating our world?

Her answers to our queries were very valuable. She told us that she was very concerned about the long term survival of fireflies not only in Thailand but in the world. She urged everyone to engage in conservation and for governments, universities, and NGOs to put up more sanctuaries to re-create their natural environment. She urged us to sponsor campaigns for the reduction of GHG emissions, carbon emissions, the rampant cutting of trees and deforestation; she called for the growing of trees, instead, and for reforestation. Only then could we continue to enjoy the flashing lights of numerous fireflies in the evening sky.

Dr. Soontorn Piromsartkoon interviewing Dr. Anchana Thancharoen regarding fireflies, April 4, 2018, in Bangkok, Thailand. Photo taken by Dr. Soontorn.

CHAPTER 11

Cold Light and Bioluminescence

We are used to thermal light, meaning, a lighted electric lamp that is hot to touch. But there is a kind of light called "cold light." This is the kind of light produced by bioluminescent organisms which is only 20% thermal heat. Why is this so? Researchers who investigated on this phenomenon of cold light noted that the light emitted by bioluminescent organisms is a result of a chemical reaction inside their bodies, unlike an electric lamp that has a filament that produces the light.

As defined by Lee (2017), bioluminescence is the "emission of light from a living organism that functions for its survival or propagation." Lee further points out that this type of light is a "cold" light resulting from a specific biochemical mechanism involving chemical processes often specific for that organism. For many, the existence of such a cold light is indeed an uncommon phenomenon.

Cold light is also known as luminescence, the type of light that is emitted when things are cold. The light emitted when things get hot is called incandescence – for example, the light from a Bunsen burner, a standard light bulb or an electric cooker. There are many types of cold light, given different names depending on the conditions under which the light is emitted (RCS, n.d.).

There is a book which is a good reference on cold light: *Cold Light: Creatures, Discoveries, and Inventions that*

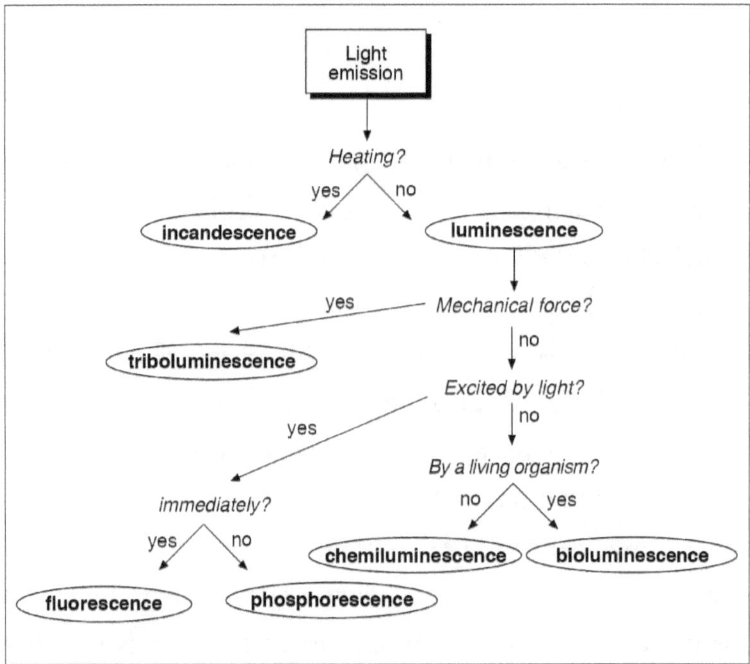

Figure 1 shows the the flow chart to decide which type of cold light an object/organism is emitting. (Source: RCS, n.d.)

Glow, by Anita Starski, published in 2007.

Cold light is defined as the chemistry of animals and things that make light but not heat (Starski, 2007). It was in 1667 when an alchemist named Robert Boyle started to do research on bioluminescence. In the process, he accidentally saw a glowing light from microorganisms on a dressed chicken left for a number of days in the kitchen. We have to remember that in those times, there was no refrigerator yet. How hard life must have been in the 1600s. How can we live without refrigerators today? But then there was Robert Boyle who had to confront a "glowing raw chicken." Yet, the chicken was not hot to the touch, so he concluded that the light coming from the bacteria that settled on the skin on the chicken was, in fact, "cold light."

What explains the presence of cold light coming from bioluminescent organisms is that bioluminescence is actually a result of a chemical reaction. When the chemical reaction happens, it releases a large amount of energy. This energy, according to Lee (2016), is so channeled as to populate the product molecule in its excitable state, instead of its being dissipated as heat like in a normal chemical reaction.

Lee (2016) further said, "This excited state is the same one produced in that molecule by the absorption of radiation, so that the spectral distribution of the bioluminescence is often the same as that of the product fluorescence."

Imagine the world when most of humanity lived a third of their day in darkness because electricity had not yet been discovered. So, in the ancient past, the people developed keen eyesight that could detect the luminescent capability of terrestrial species such as fireflies and glow-worms, rotting wood (glowing algae) and other marine bioluminescent creatures. According to Lee (2016), it was Aristotle (384-322 BCE) who was the first to recognize bioluminescence and the amazing thing was he realized that the bioluminescent light from most organisms was not accompanied by heat!

Lee (2016) pointed out that there are written records showing that Aristotle wrote about the glow from marine bioluminescent creatures, but he (Aristotle) could just describe the kind of light that they emitted. At that time, they did not know yet what bioluminescence was, and so they just described it as cold light from marine species or terrestrial organisms.

Widder (2010) remarked that oxygen is an essential requirement for the respiration of living creatures and for bioluminescence. She likewise said that the light from most bioluminescent systems could only dim but could not be extinguished. This is an amazing observation.

The reason for this light's being "perpetual" or continuous, Dr. Widder said, is because "extremely small amounts of oxygen still support the light reaction, and if oxygen is removed for some short period, the reaction precursors build up and produce a burst of reaction to luminescence when the air, or oxygen, is reintroduced."

Thus, not only having cold light but also being "perpetual" is a characteristic of bioluminescent light.

Finally, what we are doing here is making a comparison between cold light and thermal light. We can say that, on the one hand, the cold light of bioluminescent organisms is environment-friendly because it does not contribute to carbon emission. On the other hand, the thermal light such as one finds in electrical lighting systems produces heat; you can get burned or electrocuted if you touch it.

Thus, if we have the bioluminescent lighting system, such as our GlowGlobe products, then there is no way we can get burned. Suffice to say that cold light is a characteristic distinctly possessed by bioluminescent species.

CHAPTER 12

How Bioluminescence Makes A Beautiful World

Bioluminescent Creatures: Creatures of Light

The natural world is filled with creatures of light – organisms that emit bioluminescent light that are found in marine and land habitats. We find these organisms extraordinary and fascinating when we were children and until now. The fireflies inspired us to develop a disruptive innovation where we mimic their ability to produce light naturally. Of course, we can not match their natural ability to glow but we saw the possibility of using their bioluminescence to light our world.

The bioluminescent creatures are mostly found in the ocean where we can find that 90% of sea creatures at depths below 700 meters that are found to be bioluminescent.

Through the years, scientists continue to do research on these creatures of light and, as a result, more and more new bioluminescent organisms are found in the dark depths of the ocean where their production of light enables them to survive as marine species. The creation of light by these organisms are discovered is wondrous and magical and we realize that we are a part of this natural world in the entire global ecosystem.

In terrestrial habitats, fireflies are the most common bioluminescent insects known to us. Fireflies have unique ways of flashing lights to communicate and attract mates for the propagations of their species. Or, in the case of other species, they flash their lights to attract fireflies which, when lured, are eaten instead. For fireflies as creators of light, their purpose could be reproduction, defense, or deceit.

Marine Bioluminescent Light

According to Widder (2010), "The vast majority of bioluminescent organisms reside in the ocean. .". She pointed out the following information about these light-creating marine organisms that create light:

1. These bioluminescent marine organisms occupy diverse range of habitats in the ocean;

2. The ecological importance of bioluminescence in the ocean is manifest in the dominance of light emitters in open waters; and

3. Its importance is also evident in organisms that maintain functional eyes that detect bioluminescence

at a depth where there is no light that penetrates the deepest part of the ocean.

Furthermore, the habitats of these marine light emitting organisms are polar, tropical, surface waters and ocean floor. Marine scientists have been studying them for many years. According to Dr. Edith Widder, world famous expert on marine bioluminescence, in terms of light emitters, there are also varieties of these from fish, crustaceans, bacteria, and dinoflagellates.

As to the colors of the light that these organisms emit, the most dominant color is blue, followed by green color and we can find these colors among shallow coastal organisms. Very rarely do we find the colors of violet, yellow, orange and red (Widder, 2010). There are many essential questions regarding the evolutionary origins of bioluminescent creatures and scientists, like Dr. Widder, are in a race against time as marine habitats are being severely threatened by pollution, overfishing, and global climate change. There is an urgent call for all of us to save our marine habitats so that these bioluminescent species will be ensured of their long term survival.

Functions of Marine Bioluminescence

Bioluminescence can aid animal survival in at least three critical ways, according to Widder (2010). These are:

1. It can serve as an aid in locating food. For instance, they flash their light when a prey is near and they want to lure it and then lo and behold! They devour

it as food. They use their built-in headlights or flashing light to attract fish or other sea creatures which once lured, they become food and are eaten. In the deep ocean, the rule is either eat or be eaten.

2. It can be used to attract a mate. So far, this function of emitting light to attract a mate is most common among the bioluminescent creatures of the ocean and of the land, like the firefly. For the propagation and long term survival of their species, these bioluminescent creatures emit a particular flash of flight recognizable by their own species. In fact we call it the light of courtship. Once the male bioluminescent creature emits his flashing light which is recognized by the female species, then the mating takes place. However, if we expect romance in this mating practice, we will be disappointed. In the natural world, mating is instinctive and is done when the right time comes. In fact, for fireflies, the light of courtship is even more precise. We talked about it in the earlier chapters and we will again look into it when we speak of the bioluminescent organisms in the terrestrial habitats.

3. It can function as defense against predators. This, we believe, is a very important function of these creatures of light in the ocean deep. As we have earlier mentioned, down in the deep ocean, with little or no light at all that can penetrate its depth, the bioluminescent organisms are able to escape

from predators by flashing their light or blinding them with their light, whichever is more effective. It is a case of eat or be eaten, thus, predators are avoided by the marine species by emitting light which disturbs or distracts the predators with their light while trying to escape. This is part of Darwin's survival of the fittest. Those who are able to survive the predators that stalk in the ocean are able to survive. For marine bioluminescence becomes a source of defense and a way to survive for these light emitting sea creatures.

4. Marine bioluminescence serves as a source of symbiotic relationship between sea creatures and bacteria. There are luminescent bacteria that attach themselves to marine fishes and squids to form symbiotic relationship with them. The marine fishes get to have bioluminescent light in their bodies coming from the light emitting bacteria to fend off predators, to attract mate and to lure preys for food, among others. The bioluminescent bacteria on its part is able to have a host that nurtures its growth in a symbiotic environment.

The natural world, like the ocean, is filled with creatures of light. We have a beautiful world and we are a part of this global natural ecosystem. We need to ask ourselves how we can sustain the survival of the bioluminescent marine species and how humanity can save the Planet.

CHAPTER 13

How Useful is Bioluminescence?

Applications of Bioluminescent Light in Human Activities

In trying to identify the many uses of bioluminescence today, it is good to look again at the phenomenon of bioluminescence and why keen attention is currently being focused on its applications to human activities. We thus focus in this chapter on the bioluminescent light and its current uses and future applications.

According to Widder (2013), "Bioluminescence is visible light made by organisms. In the context of biophotonics, the light may be emitted by organisms, as with bacteria, or by light-producing chemicals extracted from bioluminescent organisms." She further pointed out that light in bioluminescent systems is generated by a chemical reaction and is therefore a form of chemiluminescence, hence, produced by chemical reaction.

Today, there are a number of researchers who dedicate themselves to the study of bioluminescence and how it can be applied to human activities. For instance, biologists in Columbia University are inserting genes from a bioluminescent jellyfish, Aequorea victoria, into potatoes. We know for a fact that potatoes are often watered more frequently than necessary, wasting large water quantities because of the great demand for the crop as food for countless people of the planet. This use of bioluminescence aims to solve water scarcity since the potatoes need not thereby be watered every so often and water will then be saved. These engineered potatoes would glow when exposed to black light if they needed to be watered, allowing farmers to water them only when necessary. This is an example of the application of bioluminescence in agriculture.

According to Travis and McElroy (1966), Bioluminescence research is also being conducted for its use in the medical field. Virologists Christopher Contag and Pamela Contag have begun using bioluminescent bacteria to follow the progression of infection in mice. This process could reduce the number of mice used and killed for research, since the development of the disease can be monitored when the animal is still alive (Travis and McElroy, 1966). What the researchers did was to insert bioluminescent genes into salmonella bacteria, causing them to glow. They could watch as the infection spread and could judge which antibiotics were most effective by observing the reduction in the quantity of the of the engineered bioluminescent bacteria.

There are studies that have been initiated to attempt to track the progression of the AIDS virus by changing the cells of the animal to glow when a virus is present. David Benaron, a Stanford researcher, hopes that bioluminescence will be used to track the location of cells altered by gene therapy. This research should also illustrate whether these cells, after their modification, were producing appropriate proteins.

By using firefly luciferin, biologists can ascertain the amounts of Adenine Tri-Phosphate (ATP) in plant, animal and bacterial cells. ATP acts as stored energy for these cells and is directly related to the quantity of cells present. An application of ATP indicates the incidence and amounts of bacteria present in blood or urine samples (Lee, 2016). Jellyfish aequorin which uses calcium instead of ATP for bioluminescence, may be utilized in a similar way to determine the amounts of calcium present (Biol 3211 Lecture 8-15). Bioluminescent organisms can determine toxicity because the noxious substances reduce the glow by killing the bacteria.

Most synthetic uses of bioluminescence occur in the medical field to further technological advances. Current research includes tracing the path of disease in living animals, analyzing cellular levels of ATP and calcium, thus, making advances in gene therapy. Medical professionals hope to be able to use bioluminescence research to fight AIDS, reduce the number of research animal deaths, and to improve the quality of diagnostic tests.

The following are the industry applications of bioluminescence:

1. *Green Fluorescent Protein (GFP).* This is a most important discovery in the 21st century with three scientists sharing the Nobel Prize in Chemistry in 2008 for their discovery of the photoprotein as biomarker. This was a breakthrough ten years ago. Osamu Shimamura, Martin Chalfie and Roger Tsien shared the Nobel Prize for their discovery and development of GFP. Their discovery is called glowing proteins was heralded as a guiding star in biochemistry. This was indeed a breakthrough in the use of bioluminescence in bioscience.

The remarkable brightly glowing green fluorescent protein, GFP, was first observed in the beautiful jellyfish, *Aequorea victoria* in 1962. Since then, this protein has become one of the most important tools used in contemporary bioscience. With the aid of GFP, researchers have developed ways to watch processes that were previously invisible, such as the development of nerve cells in the brain. By using DNA technology, researchers can now connect GFP to other interesting, but otherwise invisible, proteins. This glowing marker allows them to watch the movements, positions and interactions of the tagged proteins.

2. *Tourism.* Bioluminescence phenomenon has become a tourist attraction. There are a number of places in the world where tourists flock to watch bioluminescent organisms glow. For instance, the Mosquito Bay in Puerto Rico's Vieques Island is home to high concentrations of microscopic dinoflagellettes

that showcase a brilliant display of light. These are plankton organisms that create a glowing halo around anything that moves through the water. So tourists visit this area to witness the magical phenomenon. Another is the one called Bloody Wall in Cayman Island which is actually a coral wall which is home to glowing corals and bioluminescent fishes. In New Zealand, there is a mysterious cave in the Waitomo cave system where there are glowworms that drop sticky threads from their bioluminescent tails to ensnare preys. Glowworms are the larvae of beetles. This cave attracts tourists who come to watch these creatures of light.

3. *Bioluminescent imaging*– or BLI– allows for the noninvasive imaging of biological processes in living animals. Among other uses, this makes it possible to study the processes of various diseases and of treatments for those diseases. It can also be used to locate tumors.

According to Widder (2013), Bioluminescent Imaging has revolutionized infectious diseases studies by making it possible to track the course of an infection in a single animal. Researchers need not then spend so much time and employ so many cohorts to do the infectious disease studies since the BLI enables them to do it at one time.

4. *Bioluminescent Resonance Energy Transfer,* or BRET, is used to map neuronal circuits in order to understand brain function.

5. *Quorum sensing.* Studies on bioluminescence among bacteria in sea water led to the discovery of what is known as quorum sensing. J. W. Hastings and E. P. Greenberg

reported in the Journal of Bacteriology in May 1999 that at low cell densities, the luciferase gene was not transcribed, but luminescent genes do activate at high cell densities when the light emitted is bright enough to serve a purpose. It is now accepted that cell-cell communication in bacteria is common.

6. *Tools* have been developed that use bioluminescence in many ways. Since adenosine triphosphate (ATP), an energy storing molecule found in all living cells, is required for the emission of light, the amount of light is directly proportional to the amount of ATP. Measurements of ATP can therefore detect contamination far more quickly and accurately than traditional culturing. An example of a tool that does this is the BioScan made by GE. This small instrument measures bacteria in water simply and almost immediately (Travis and McElroy, 1966).

7. *Nature Lamps.* This was mentioned by Professor Stevani where there were attempts to use bioluminescent algae as a source of light for the lamp. But this is maybe a crude way compared with the process in which our invention is anchored. But there is the usual skepticism among scientists whether future innovations for lighting systems using bioluminescence could be achieved. And whether, if at all achievable, the cost considerations might defeat the purpose of its business potential.

PART FOUR

Bioluminescent Light: A Disruptive Innovation

CHAPTER 14

Industrial Revolution 4.0

Fourth Industrial Revolution: What we Need to Know

There is a buzz word today called Industry 4.0 and those countries who participated in the recent World Economic Forum 2017 talked about this Fourth Industrial Revolution to the nth power, but ordinary citizens are wondering what is the fuss all about? Of course, for most of the uninitiated, they could not care less and they go about their daily lives as if today will still be the same by tomorrow.

But it is important for us to know what this new economic engine they call Industry 4.0 is all about because whether we like it or not, it will affect us one way or the other today and in the foreseeable future. In fact, our lives today are already being affected by this emerging economic phenomenon without our being aware of it – through the Internet of Things (IoT), the artificial intelligence (AI) in the manufacturing sector, the 3D printing, and the digital businesses sprouting like mushrooms, not to mention nanotechnology and synthetic biology, and biotechnology, among other technological breakthroughs.

Let us imagine a day without our mobile phones, our Internet access, our online shopping, our computers from laptops, iPads, tablets and other digital gadgets. We will certainly be so upset because they have become our new normal. It is unthinkable to be deprived of them in a day!

What is the Fourth Industrial Revolution?

Simply put, the Fourth Industrial Revolution is the next economic engine and it focuses on technology and innovation for the future of production. It is expected that by 2025, productivity will create value up to $3.7 trillion worldwide (WEF, 2017). If we think about this prediction, it is staggering. But this is just a prediction. It will not happen if in the next seven years, we can not scale up and diffuse the technology in the world ecosystem. This needs the collaborations of many stakeholders.

These technologies are those that make our lives easier today, like Internet of Things (IoT), advanced robotics, Artificial Intelligence, machine learning, nanotechnology, biotechnology, additive manufacturing, among other cutting edge technologies that are revolutionizing the way we manufacture products. The IoT has given us digital businesses and allows for "connecting and tracking asset performance in real time, as well as for integrating production and consumption processes." (WEF, 2017). This online integration of processes from production to consumption shortens the lead time and enables faster production and reaches consumers likewise more quickly.

The World Economic Forum System Initiative on Shaping the Future of Production provides "a platform for leaders across the public and private sectors to work together to build a more inclusive and sustainable future of production." It can be noted that in pursuing this goal, the stakeholders look to technology and innovation to boost economic growth, and to promote a human-centered approach for the benefit of all.

Pilot Purgatory

The world leaders have a funny label for those companies in the industry sectors that are still in the "Pilot Stage." They are still experimenting in their factories on the new technologies and are said to be stuck up in the "Pilot Purgatory" where technology is deployed experimentally at a reduced scale for an extended period due to the inability or lack of conviction to roll it out at production-system scale. Without the scaling and diffusion of technology, there can be no increase of productivity and things remain as experiments. Businesses should move from the pilot stage to adopting technology at scale in order to benefit from increased productivity.

Today, this is not yet happening so there is the need for collaborations among industry sectors, governments, and businesses to scale up. The Industry 4.0 will not move forward to its goal of increasing productivity through technology and innovation across industry sectors and countries if there are no such collaborations that create the enabling ecosystem for Industry 4.0.

Two years ago, in 2016, the World Economic Forum established the System's Initiative Framework and today it has become more diverse and counts over 60 businesses from 18 industry sectors, 25 ministers of commerce and/or industry, and representatives from top engineering universities, labor unions and civil society organizations.

Within the System Initiative's framework, the Technology and Innovation for the Future of Production project, developed in collaboration with McKinsey & Company, is exploring how industrial companies can take technology adoption in production from proof of concept to industrial scale.

Emerging Technologies and Innovations in the Fourth Industrial Revolution

To understand Industry 4.0, we would like to raise some fundamental questions for the emerging technologies and seek answers to our queries.

Where are we now?

The first question we would like to ask rhetorically

is, where are we now? When we consider technology and innovation, we are at the cusp of a great industrial revolution but we cannot appreciate it unless we look at what we have at present and look back to the past that brought us today. So many dedicated scientists have spent their lifetimes to make discoveries and inventions and they have been so busy inventing that they have no time to reflect on the impact of their inventions. So, we will do the reflection for them.

First we look at the invention of the airplane. We ride on an airplane like say a Jumbo Jet and we never bother to reflect on how on earth some people made it possible for us to undertake a transatlantic flight? We stay too long up in the air and we doze off or read a book and wait for our arrival at the airport of destination. In short, we take for granted this invention and who invented it, which has enabled us until today to reach faraway places on Earth. If we look back in history, it was Leonardo da Vinci, yes, the famous Italian artist, who started to make sketches of birds in flight. Then, it was the Wright Brothers who finally invented the airplane. On hindsight, if these inventors did not take time to study the birds and pigeons, we would probably still be going places by horsedrawn carriages.

Now, we look at today and ask where are we currently in terms of aviation? We have rockets and we have drones and spaceships. We are able to send people to the moon or to the international space station as a space traveller (if one can afford the exorbitant price in millions of dollars of a round trip ticket by spaceship). The Fourth Industrial Revolution will send humans to Mars, thanks to Elon Musk and his BIG dream of colonizing the Red Planet. In the past when Elon Musk was thinking about going to Mars, he was mocked, ridiculed, laughed at and called crazy. Today, Elon Musk has commercial spacecrafts being rented out to the US government to bring supply to the astronauts manning the space stations.

Let us consider also the service robots today. In the past, these robots belonged to the realm of science fiction by our favorite author Isaac Asimov. Or in the Star Trek movie from the imagination of George Lucas. It was unthinkable then that robots would overtake us in their smartness and their ability to surpass human intelligence. But today, we know that the industry sectors make use of robots to do repetitive and mundane tasks.

Then we have Artificial Intelligence and Machine Learning which are also just science fiction in the past. Today AI is applied in the manufacturing sectors, and in many other types of industries which run our trains, our factories, and many other things.

In the field of medicine, many technology-driven innovations are assisting our medical professionals to provide quality care to their patients such as use of biotechnology, synthetic biology, nanotechnology, as well as gene re-engineering, to name a few. But these technological innovations were non-existent say 50 years ago.

In various fields of endeavors, technology and innovation are the driving factors of modern progress today. So, our next fundamental question is, where are we going, with all these being available to us for the improvement of our lives?

Where are we heading?

The latest novel of Dan Brown, *Origin* (Brown, 2017) asks two fundamental questions about humanity. Where did we come from and where are we going? He deals with a supercomputer who dominates the mind of the main character so much so that it is all-pervasive and the computer is just in the cell phone and its central location is in Spain. It is an exciting novel if only for the glimpse it gives us of an imagined future.

In the conversations we are having about the Fourth Industrial Revolution, the second fundamental question we ask is "where are we heading?" This is the same question raised by Dan Brown (2017). Where is humanity going?

Given the advances in technology and the innovations happening all around us today, where are all of these technological innovations leading us? Into what kind of future? And is this future for all, an inclusive economic growth for all industries and all countries, big or small across the world?

Technology and innovation will remain the main drivers of this new economic engine, for sure. But how can these technologies of production be scaled up and not remain as "experiments," eventually dying a natural death for lack of motivation of companies to scale and diffuse these new technologies? And what about the small and medium enterprises (SMEs)? How will they cope with the megatrends? Given their limited resources and their size, they might be left in the wayside while large companies have moved on, scaling up and diffusing the new technologies across industries?

In the context of the Fourth Industrial Revolution, production is at the cusp of the paradigm shift driven by the three technological megatrends pointed out by McKinsey & Company (WEF, 2017), namely:

Key technology megatrends transforming production
Connectivity

This megatrend creates links between discrete network nodes, increasing visibility. When we talk of connectivity of course we are talking about the Internet! How can we survive a day without Internet access? Connectivity is fast expanding through what we call Internet of Things (IoT). These IoT platforms are transforming the way industries' assets are connected to production. What will happen is that through IoT platforms, production and consumption processes will be integrated and linked so closely together so that consumers get the products and services they need in real time.

Major technology companies see the opportunity to invest heavily in hyper-scalable IoT platforms and we can predict that in 2025, connectivity in the industry sector will be at its height. We are heading towards global scale in terms of connectivity with 8.4 billion devices connected so that companies all over the world are in fact interconnected in a global supply chain and their customers will be highly visible and interactive in the production process, getting the product they want and when they need it.

Intelligence

This megatrend pertains to the ability to automate event recognition and translation for decision-making. We are talking here of Artificial Intelligence which has reached awesome power in its ability to reach the accuracy of the human brain, and if left unchecked, in the near future, it will surpass human intelligence, and what will happen to us mere mortals and not machines? Will we aspire for immortal life so that we can match the ability of machines or computers to go on forever and ever? What shall we be occupying ourselves with when Artificial Intelligence will perform most of the tasks we, humans,are supposed to be doing? Shall we be rendered redundant by robots or shall we evolve into higher spiritual beings engaging in the finer things of life such as music, culture, and the arts?

Indeed, when we come to think of it, the Fourth Industrial Revolution will bring both great benefits and great risks to humankind. Where are we heading given the advances in the computing power of robots and their ability to reach speech and image recognition like that of the human brain? There will be a need to re-design the school curriculum to teach our kids not to do computer programming or Math but to engage in music, painting, and the arts, finer things in life that will increase their level of human consciousness and where they can excel when compared to Artificial Intelligence. For after all, we, humans, are the creators of these robots, and we do have leaps of intelligence that no machine can match in the foreseeable future. We should never allow the robots to conquer us, and be enslaved by them. But, we can never tell, so this is the great risk that goes with AI.

Machine learning like artificial neural networks, fuzzy logic, genetic algorithms, and working with Big Data is used to engage in disruptive innovation. That is, to use Big Data analytics processes trillions of information available in the databases of Facebook and Twitters, as well as other digital platforms and social media that churn out trillions and trillions of Big Data for purposes of decision making. Huge profits are thus at stake for those who know how to make sense of Big Data. That is the secret of Mark Zuckerberg, Bill Gates, and Jeff Bezos, among others, who own social media networks.

Currently, the potential of artificial intelligence has not yet been maximized by the industry. Only very few firms are making use of Big Data for decision making in production. However, this may change in the next few years once companies will realize how they can leverage using machine learning.

Flexible automation

Flexible automation incorporates response mechanisms, automation and remote movement. This pertains to automation technology in the manufacturing sector. Currently, not all companies have automated their production processes, even in highly industrialized countries, like South Korea. It was mentioned in WEB 2017 that there are only 530 robots per 10,000 production workers deployed, which is still a very low penetration level. How much more for those developing countries where the costs of acquiring industrial robots may be very prohibitive. But in the next 10 years, this scenario will change. Scaling up and diffusion will be the solution to the low penetration level of automation technology.

What are our drivers for this future?

In the context of the Fourth Industrial Revolution, the number one driver of this economic engine will be technology and the subsequent innovations that will arise from these technologies. Thus, technology and innovation will be the drivers of this future as defined by the Fourth Industrial Revolution. This revolution will occur in the context of production and how productivity can be increased significantly through the application of new technologies such as artificial intelligence and machine learning.

Other drivers of this future will be the world leaders who will take up the challenge of instituting the right economic climate and enabling ecosystem in their countries to adopt the technologies that drive productivity as part of their reinventing of their factories.

Ultimately, the inventors and innovators of new technologies will be the major drivers of the Fourth Industrial Revolution because without them, there will be no new technologies that will be invented in the next 50 years until 2100.

A strong venture capital industry for technological startups will be a driver of this desired future. Without the investing industry, innovators will have a hard time sustaining their startups until these can stand on their own.

For the academe, a culture of science will drive inventions and innovations since new ideas will come from the young, given the right training and motivation for excellence.

What could the future look like?

For Industry 4.0, robots will be so far advanced that humans will be rendered redundant; robots will then take over most jobs that humans used to do. This will cause a big headache for all employers and employees and new skills have to be developed along with creativity and innovation, because workers will have to do more innovative thinking, being freed from the drudgery of their routine tasks.

Brains as computers – computers as brains – these have become interchangeable. Artificial intelligence is now poised to surpass human intelligence. In the Year 2100, AI will become so powerful that it will take over all of the tasks that humans can perform, except those involving emotions and those wonderful leaps of intelligence that only humans can do. What should we do about this? The best thing to do is to prepare and be ready for a life dominated by robots and to start acquiring the new skills that artificial intelligence cannot do which will be in the area of the arts, such as music, poetry, painting, and other emerging cultural forms for the purpose of enobling the life of a human being.

In some sense, the future has already arrived somewhere, but not maybe in our own countries or places of work. The ultimate goal is for the improvement of the lives of our people, particularly, those who have long been victims of capability deprivations – the marginalized poor who are still mired in poverty – despite the wealth and economic progress of developed nations. The Industry 4.0 should aim for inclusive growth for all people in the world by addressing the triple bottom line of people, planet and profit.

How do we achieve our desired future?

It may not be easy nor will it be quick, but it is important for us to know our desired future and that we are able to dream BIG and act small. Transformations in most cases bring with them challenges and risks. So, we should be well prepared for meeting the challenges that will come our way. The desirable future is not only for our present generation but for those many generations yet to come.

In order for us to achieve our desired future, we need to act now and not wait for the future which will never come unless we take the initiatives to turn our dreams into a reality. We need to be positive thinkers and believe in ourselves, believe in what we desire, in what we can achieve. Lastly, and more importantly, we need to promote a human-centred approach for the benefit of all.

A Case of an Emerging Digital Tourism Platform:

TOECHOK CO., LTD

"Preparations for the company launch have already been made and the countdown has started before the big event," said Dr. Soontorn. "I am optimistic we will be able to achieve our targets of penetrating initially the Asian tourism market."

With his usual optimism and enthusiasm for the business, Dr. Soontorn Piromsartkoon, CEO and Chief Marketing Officer of Toechok Co. Ltd was discussing the future of the startup with his two Co-Founders. The launch will be held three months from now in Phuket Island, Thailand. Many guests and stakeholders, including the media of Bangkok, have been invited to the event. The Management Team is looking at the prospects of achieving their goal of "An all-inclusive Platform for Tourism" through digital business. They are aware that the Internet of Things (IoT) has enabled many companies to have an online presence.

His two Co-Founders, on the contrary, are having some doubts if indeed they can hit their profit targets given the stiff competition in the tourism industry among the ASEAN countries. Three years ago, they began their journey with the startup company and now they are about to make the plunge. Will they make it? What will be the drivers of success for a digital business model such as that of Toechok?

Toechok Co., Ltd was established on November 30,

Namchok Petsaen, Chief Technology Officer and Co-founder of Toechok Co., Ltd., in Bangkok, Thailand. Photo taken by Dr. Soontorn Piromsartkoon, May 4, 2018.

2016 in Bangkok, Thailand. It is a privately held company founded by Dr. Soontorn Piromsartkoon, Namchok Petaen, and Narong Mongtom. The purpose of this business is to provide a tourism network in the form of a web platform to promote tourism contents, services and products for travel agencies, tour operators, travellers, and tour guides along with the promotion of travel accessories and souvenir products as well as a restaurant management system, transportation rental, accommodation, and recreational activities (hereafter called "Toechok Platform"). In addition, there are specific tourism contents/products/services for people with disabilities and the elderly.

Company Background

In 2013 Bunraksar Travel Co. Ltd was established in Bangkok, Thailand as a tour operating company arranging both inbound and outbound travel. Due to the increasing popularity of online bookings worldwide, a few years later the management took further steps of establishing tour packages online as a platform called Toechok (www.toechok.com) which is developed by Toechok Co. Ltd. Four years later, it spinned off as a digital startup offering an online web tourism platform.

The services of Toechok consist of the following :

1. Booking engine and e-commerce system for Toechok platform
2. Tracking mechanism of bookings
3. Statistical reports
4. Travel society for creating and sharing travel contents in Toechok network by member users/travelers
5. Newsletter and Subscription
6. Advertising programs
7. Customer management system.

The Toechok platform will have access to the website where they can 1) provide their own profiles and contents; 2) load their own products/services and prices; 3) manage their own advertising program for particular groups of customers, and 4) create and share travel contents in Toechok network by member users/travelers.

These are planned to be provided by stages or phases.

The Business Model

Toechok Co., Ltd has two business models: Transactions and Advertisement. Transaction business model is one of B2B (lands to travel agencies, tour operator, travel accessories, souvenirs, tourism contents) to B2C (users, travellers and shoppers). Its advertisement model is designed to promote by way of contents/services/products, keywords, email, and banner advertisements within Toechok platform and further facilitate search engines for the travel agencies, tour operators, souvenirs, tourism contents, and travel accessories.

Tourism Industry in Thailand

There is a large global market for this business and tourism is a major economic force in Thailand. The world average of direct contribution of Travel & Tourism to GDP in 2015 was USD 2,229.8 billion (3.0% of GDP). This primarily reflects the economic activity generated by industries such as hotels, travel agents, airlines and other passenger transportation services (excluding commuter services). But it also includes, for example, the activities of the restaurant and leisure industries directly supported by the business.

The global average of total contribution of Travel & Tourism to GDP (including wider effects from investment, the supply chain and induced income impacts) was USD 7,170.3 billion in 2015 (9.8% of GDP). It is forecast to rise by 4.0% pa to USD 10,986.5 billion by 2026 (10.8% of GDP).

In addition, Bangkok is a crossroad of international air transport. The hotel and retail industry have expanded due to the demand in travel arrangements. According to The World Travel & Tourism Council (WTTC) 2016 Report, the direct contribution of Travel & Tourism in Thailand to GDP in 2015 was THB 1,247.3 billion (9.3% of GDP). This primarily reflects the economic activity generated by industries such as hotels, travel agents, airlines and other passenger transportation services (excluding commuter services). But it also includes, for example, the activities of the restaurant and leisure industries directly supported by the business. The direct contribution of Travel & Tourism to GDP is expected to grow by 6.7% pa to THB 2,482.9 billion (14.0% of GDP) by 2026.

Disruptive Innovation in the Global Tourism Industry

The Toechok Co., Ltd is considered a disruptive innovation under the tourism industry and it needs to understand why and how to handle this reality. The traditional business model for tourism has been to have independent online travel and tours companies which compete under e-commerce. Creating a web tourism platform disrupts the current way of doing business. The business model is all-inclusive and cuts across many tourism services, causing creative destruction along its path.

How shall Toechok Co., Ltd handle the following:

1. The exponential growth that will happen when the company graduates as a startup and is fully integrated in an intricate web tourism network, as reflected below:

"The purpose of this business is to provide a tourism network in the form of a web platform to promote tourism contents, services and products for travel agencies, tour operators, travellers, and tour guides along with the promotion of travel accessories and souvenir products as well as a restaurant management system, transportation rental, accommodation, and recreational activities."

2. The organizational expansion to be done from startup to fully functioning corporation with the needed staff, updated IT and other technologies, mobile apps, website expansion, etc.?

3. Where will the revenue streams come from and how will these be realized ?

CHAPTER 15

Why Disruptive Innovation?

Introduction

One of the main topics of this book, aside from the phenomenon of bioluminescence, is disruptive innovation. We consider our bioluminescent lighting system, GlowGlobe, as a disruptive innovation of the future. Why is this so? What makes our invention a disruptive product? What will our product disrupt in the market?

Ever since Christensen (1995) introduced the management concept of disruptive innovation, he has expanded the concept in more than two decades. His disruptive innovation model has been used in business schools worldwide. We will see how his model works and how we can turn disruptive innovation to our advantage when competing in the market. In the free market forces, those companies which refuse to innovate will be wiped out or will be crushed by the more innovative companies. The market does not care whether the company is large, mature and stable; it is brutal in the sense that it allows free forces to dictate the market movements. A new but highly innovative entrant in terms of products or services will create not only ripples but storms in the market, disrupting the way things are currently done. Thus, disruptive innovation is the way to compete and survive the competition.

Creative Destruction

All disruptive innovations spring from what is termed by Schumpeter (1934, cited in Khanser, 2007: 8) as "Creative Destruction." This process pertains to the "never ending cycle of creation and destruction of enterprises across markets and industries." This means that the innovative companies simultaneously create new products and business models and eliminate others. Entrepreneurs are always on the lookout for business opportunities or new ideas or inventions in order to convert these into successful innovations. The creation and destruction processes happen more swiftly in the market than in companies (Foster and Kaplan, 2001).

Hansen (2010) in his study on disruptive innovations and business models used Foster and Kaplan's (2001) concept of "creative destruction." Hansen noted that this book on creative destruction draws a lot of data from The McKinsey Corporate Performance Database which contains detailed data from more than 1,000 US companies. Therefore, it is also a book to use when studying the phenomenon of disruptive innovation.

Disruptive Innovation Defined

So, what is the theory of disruptive innovation? According to Christensen, Raynor and McDonald (2016), disruption is "a process whereby a smaller company with fewer resources is able to successfully challenge established incumbent businesses." The authors further pointed out that disruptive innovation occurs at the lower–end market, consisting of those customers unserved by the established companies which are very busy doing improvements to their products and services to satisfy their most profitable customers. Disruption happens when the new entrant, usually a small company or a startup, gains foothold in those unserved markets, offering many functionalities which are simple to use, very convenient, and, of course, cheaper than the current products. The disruptor moves upmarket and begins to capture the mainstream customers; at this instance, disruption has occurred.

Likewise, Hansen (2010) pointed out that disruptive innovations do not aim to bring better products to high-end customers; instead they disrupt the market by introducing products and services that are not as good as the current products. So they enter the low-end market and slowly improve on their innovation until such a time when they are able to capture the more established high-end market; the cycle of creation and destruction thus begins.

It has to be noted that disruption is not a one time deal. It takes time since it is a process. For instance, when Jack Ma (Clark, 2016) disrupted the Chinese retail market with his e-retailer, Alibaba, ten years ago, it was a slow process of moving from the inner cities of China into the big cities like Beijing and Shanghai. Jack Ma's strategy then was to offer quick delivery of goods to those Chinese customers who bought online and who had no access to big retail stores. Jack Ma as a disruptor is the man behind the innovative, and highly successful, e-commerce revolution in the largest nation on the planet. Alibaba currently presides over 70% of the Chinese e-retail market (Clark, 2016). His e-commerce model is a disruptive innovation model and many did not think it would succeed. But today, it's the biggest e-retailer in the world.

Disruptors tend to focus on getting the business model, rather than merely the product, just right. (Christensen, Raynor and McDonald, 2016) When they succeed, their movement from the fringe (the low end of the market or a new market) to the mainstream erodes first the incumbents' market share and then their profitability.

Model of Disruptive Innovation

Christensen (1995) has developed a model of disruptive innovation that has become the basis for business analysis. It has three components or elements, namely, the rate of improvement the customer can absorb, the pace of technological progress, and the distinction between sustaining and disruptive innovation. Let us look into each of these elements.

The Rate of Improvement the Customer can Absorb

For this particular element, Christensen's model says that the disruptive innovation is way beyond what the customer can absorb. An example that we can look at is the electric car of Elon Musk (Vance, 2017).It is a disruptive innovation that does away with gasoline to fuel a car. But at the moment, the price of an electric car is still very prohibitive. Besides, even with an electric car, a customer will still have to deal with traffic jam, speed limits and safety issues. Thus, only a few customers are able to afford an electric car and they remain in the fringes of the market.

But if we give Elon Musk 10 years, his car will have moved to the mainstream market and the well-established car companies will have to innovate or else they will face tough competition with the disruptive car product. The same experience we also have with our desktop computers, then laptop, then notebook, then iPad, then iPhone. These were considered disruptive products and ultimately they moved to mainstream market when customers begin to absorb the improvements on their computers. At this time the disruptor gains the upperhand and begins to dominate the market and wipe out the competition.

The Pace of Technological Progress

The winds of technological change today may be strong,

given Industrial Revolution 4.0. But the customers may not yet be ready with the fast rate of technological progress. When a disruptive innovation enters the market, it enters the low-end segment where the unserved customers are waiting to try new products and services. According to Christensen, Raynor and McDonald (2016), "it is important to notice that in almost every industry the rate of the technological progress is higher than the rate of performance that customers can utilize or absorb."

Distinction between Sustaining and Disruptive Innovation

There are two kinds of innovation that are competing here, what Christensen (1995) calls sustaining innovation and disruptive innovation. The two types differ in the way innovation is approached. For sustaining innovation, the company aims at very demanding high-end customers and what the company does is to improve on the products and continuously engage in incremental improvements year by year. So efforts are on the current product offering and no new innovation is made although it may happen that the company is able to make technological breakthroughs. But in sustaining innovation, it is always the well-established competitors that win because they are ahead of everybody in the competition while the new entrant is struggling with its product innovation and trying to sustain its performance.

On the other hand, disruptive innovators are not so much concerned about targeting the high-end customers as about disrupting the market with disruptive technologies that offer benefits to the low-end customers. Furthermore, there are customers in the market who are on the lookout for innovative products and are willing to try these out. They usually are less demanding customers or they belong to a new market segment that prefer disruptive or alternative products. Thus, as the disruptors continue to improve their products, these become more satisfying to their customers until such a time that they become the preferred product over the old product. At this point, the companies engaged in sustaining innovation will not be able to deal with the disruptive innovation since the latter has already gained the mainstream market.

The Challenges of Disruptive Innovations in the Market

We, as authors of this book, consider ourselves as disruptive technology innovators and we understand that there are a number of challenges facing us today as we bring our disruptive product in the market.

The journey towards creating high growth products is not easy. This is even more arduous for new entrants who have to compete with established companies which have already captured the high-end customers. Nevertheless, disruptive innovations can still ease them out of the competition.

If we trace the journey of a disruptive innovation, the product starts from a raw idea, develops into a new business idea, and then it goes through a series of processes where the business idea is modified, enhanced, and shaped into a viable product idea that can be funded. For most startups, this will come from venture capital funding. If it does not show promise of commercialization, then it will be discontinued and fade away in oblivion. Such is the way of an idea; it will either flourish or die a natural death. Hence, a lean startup will do better in such a situation of uncertainty, because it can pivot with ease if need be (Ries, 2011). If the idea shows business potential, then it goes through the prototyping, then the testing of the market, then finally its commercialization as a disruptive innovation.

What is innovation?

There is a way to understand what innovation is, and that is by examining the Innovation Chain presented by Foxon et al (2008), who in turn adopted the innovation chain process from Grubb (2004).

Innovation starts with Early Research. Like the basic research that scientists are doing, making new discoveries in their laboratory, we also go through the process of conducting experiments in a laboratory to develop our prototype. Most of the results of scientists' experiments have no commercial value at the time they come out of the laboratory and the product is considered just as a new discovery. Only through an enterprising individual who sees its commercial potential can an innovation spring from the raw idea.

The next step in the innovation process is demonstration and commercialization. When the new knowledge is applied to the real world, then it goes though piloting, demonstrating, and becoming a maiden commercial-scale project. At this stage of the journey, there is a need for venture capitalists and for other funding institutions to come in and infuse venture capital for the full commercialization of the disruptive innovation. If the project proves to be not viable, it will fall into what technopreneurs call the "valley of death", meaning, it fails commercially.

The last step in the innovation process is market uptake. When the disruptive product is proven commercially viable, it is introduced to the market and it competes with the rest of the old products and disrupt their existence.

Why do Firms Need Disruptive Innovation?

While the mindset of companies favors the continuity of their products and services over a long term of sustainability, the market prefers discontinuity. It welcomes creative destruction because it is the best way to destroy old products and create new ones. The cycle of creation and destruction keeps the market alive. As we mentioned earlier in this book, the market is brutal. It thrives on the principle of the survival for the fittest in the jungle we call market. Thus, we ask ourselves: Is there a market for our disruptive product? Who are our customers? In the final analysis, those who innovate will ride the waves of creative destruction.

CHAPTER 16

Biotechnology and Bioluminescent Light

"The biggest innovation of the twenty-first century will be the intersection of technology and biology. A new era is beginning."
- Steve Jobs (Issacson, 2011)

An Overview of Biotechnology

We include in this book the topic on biotechnology and how it is related to the phenomenon of bioluminescence because, to fully understand the bioluminescent lighting system we are developing, we need to know the role of biotechnology in the production of bioluminescent light sans electricity.

As defined, biotechnology is a technology combined with biology. In other words, it is technology based on biology. This means that biotechnology makes use of cellular and biomolecular processes to develop technologies and products that will improve the lives of people on Planet Earth. For more than 6,000 years, many scientists have made discoveries on how the biological processes of microorganisms can be harnessed as technological products in the areas of food, health, medicine, agriculture, and the reduction of carbon footprint through renewable energy, among others.

Today, biotechnology covers many different disciplines, e.g. genetics, biochemistry, and molecular biology, among others. New technologies and new products are developed every year within the areas of medicine (new medicines and therapies), agriculture (genetically modified plants, biofuels, biological treatment), and industrial biotechnology (production of chemicals, paper, textiles and food).

For instance, the cheese products we enjoy are a product of biotechnology, and the bread that we love to eat makes use of yeast to make the dough grow. The yogurt products that are being marketed have live bacteria in them (at least, they are the good bacteria). Our biofuels come from the renewable biomass of organic waste and this helps reduce carbon footprint and greenhouse gas emissions.

If we come to think of it, there are many biotechnological products that have been developed for our use and we just take them for granted. Have we ever paused to consider how these biotechnological products have been made? Because of biotechnology, more than 250 health care products have been manufactured to cure some illnesses and diseases; patients all over the world are benefited by these medicines.

Today, farmers worldwide, more than 14 million of them, are benefiting from biotechnology's ability to help improve the yield of their crops, pest control, and many other aspects of farming. Modern agriculture makes use of biotechnology to improve farming methods through biotechnology techniques. With the development of genetic engineering in the 1970's, research in biotechnology has flourished because of the possibility of making changes in the organism's genetic material, its DNA. This was the discovery of Watson and Crick, and was popularized in a book, titled *The Double Helix* (Watson, 1968). They won the Nobel Prize for their discovery of the DNA in 1962.

Bioluminescent Light and Biotechnology

In Chapter 15, we presented some of the challenges of disruptive innovation. This time, we will look into the innovation challenges of bioluminescent light as a disruptive innovation, in particular the challenges in the application of biotechnology while creating living light. We know for a fact that bioluminescent light is light created by some species through some kind of chemical reaction in their bodies. We would like at this point to show the link between bioluminescent light and biotechnology.

How can biotechnology be applied to the phenomenon of bioluminescence?

While in the past, there were doubts on the potential of bioluminescence to light our world, today new innovations and inventions as well as new designs using biotechnology and synthetic biology are making headway and soon we will be able to use lamps fueled by bioluminescence. We will have streets and avenues lined with glowing trees lighting our way. We will be saying goodbye to electric lamps and electric lamp posts. We will no longer need electric outlets for our indoor lighting systems. We are excited about this future and we strongly believe that while these innovations can be disruptive, such bioluminescent lighting systems will be the living light of the future.

Bioluminescence Technology: Its Future

The question we ask now is this: Is there a future for bioluminescence technology? We do believe that the future is bright for bioluminescence technology. It is about time that we make use of this natural source of light we call "living light" to transform current mindsets about how we can light the world using biological source.

In the previous chapters of this book, we introduce some of the companies that are into developing bioluminescent light for possible use as an alternative source of light. These are the following:

Taxa Biotechnologies (USA). This startup company is trying to produce glowing trees. By genetically modifying the DNA of plants, the company hopes to see the plants glowing as bioluminescent trees. The goal is to have these glowing trees line the streets and avenues of the future.

Glowee Company (France) likewise develops a biological source of light, using the natural properties of marine microorganisms. The founder of the startup company said that their goal is to disrupt the way we produce and consume light by offering a living and self-sufficient lighting with a raw material that requires no installation infrastructure.

A **Professor of MIT, USA,** together with his team, is also into glowing plants. They were able to produce a glowing watercress plant, but its light is short-lived. Again, the challenge is how to prolong the duration of bioluminescent light.

The fourth startup company is our own **Perpetual Light Biotechnologies** with its GlowGlobe product. We have Chapter 18 devoted to our disruptive innovation on bioluminescent lighting system as a case study.

Innovation Challenges of Bioluminescent Light

We can see that there are a number of challenges that all of us researchers and scientists are currently facing in our attempt to come up with bioluminescent lighting systems and materials for commercialization.

A major challenge is the duration of the bioluminescent light. All researchers are having problems on how to achieve longer duration of the bioluminescent light. Further experiments may yield a solution to this major problem. If the solution is found, this will surely be a big contribution in the attempt to commercialize bioluminescent lighting.

Another innovation challenge of bioluminescence biotechnology has to do with the risks of synthetic biology. How to mitigate these risks is taken up in Chapter 16 of this book.

Because we are dealing with bacteria, microbes, or microorganisms that are genetically modified to produce light, we must ensure that these are friendly bacteria or else we will run the risk of pandemic or other unwarranted infections.

The effects on our ecosystem of genetically modified microorganisms serving as hosts in the production of bioluminescent light may be hard to predict. Hence, we need to exercise care in the application of biotechnology to bioluminescence.

CHAPTER 17

Synthetic Biology: Benefits and Risks

An Overview of Synthetic Biology

In Chapter 16, we saw the link between bioluminescence and biotechnology and how the two play an important role in the development of the lighting systems from bioluminescence. This time we will look into synthetic biology which is closely related to biotechnology. We need to understand this concept because it is very central to the disruptive innovation of our perpetual lighting system using bioluminescence.

We define synthetic biology as the application of engineering principles to biology in order to design and construct novel and biological systems for specific applications, such as on bioluminescent organisms, especially for the development of living light. We know that we have been altering the genetic code of plants and animals for thousands of years by selectively breeding the individual plants or animals with desirable features. With the discovery of the DNA by Watson and Crick, biotechnologists can now acquire a genetic information associated with some useful features of an organism and transfer or add it to another organism. This is the basis of genetic engineering. We can now read and manipulate genetic code in order to develop better organisms. Because we now understand how natural biological systems grow and evolve, we now have the capability to develop new breeds of plants and animals through genetic engineering. We believe that this is an exciting technology combined with biology, chemistry, using engineering and computer programming techniques.

The essence is that new biological systems and organisms are created or designed through genetic modification. It looks like synthetic biology allows us to re-design life.

There are two camps of scientists in the debate of whether synthetic biology is a new discipline or just a type of systems biology, meaning, simply an extension of already existing methods of genetic engineering. We are told that the key distinction that defines synthetic biology is the ability to build from the ground up using engineering and computer programming techniques. Traditional genetic engineering takes existing DNA and inserts DNA from another organism to create rDNA (recombinant DNA). This time, with the availability of 3D printers and gene laboratories and computing power, synthetic biology will allow researchers to create DNA strands which are not found in the natural world.

Accordingly, synthetic biology techniques will allow us to build the base pair sequences from component parts and assemble them from scratch.

What makes it possible for us to redesign microorganisms for some purpose other than what they naturally do?

Engineering is the key to synthetic biology. It allows the integration of biology, chemistry and information technology to fit into a model that will enable innovations to happen. However, we also need to look into the risks that may be unwittingly caused by this combination of various fields. Synthetic biology is a new and exciting technology but there are still many areas we need to understand about it.

It is synthetic biology that is enabling us bioluminescent researchers to undertake pioneering work on lighting systems using bioluminescence. It will take genetically re-engineered microorganisms to emit light. Arguably, these genetically modified microbes will be doing what is not natural for them and thus they will be modifying or mimicking nature. An instance would be if there will be attempts to produce glowing plants to serve as lighting for streets and avenues. The genetically modified plants will behave like those bioluminescent organisms we mentioned in the previous chapters of this book. They will glow in the dark. However, these trees and plants in the natural world are not supposed to emit light. Hence, they have been re-designed for a purpose not natural for them. If plants have memories, they will recall that they are not supposed to emit light, and they might resist.

It would be interesting to observe how the glowing plants will react to the genetic modification.

What is Synthetic Biology?

It is important to know that it is in the process of creating life from natural and synthetic building blocks by which synthetic biology begins to follow diverse directions. One query is this: Which parts of life are the building blocks and which are its essence of life? We could, for instance, argue that life is in the genomes, and the whole phenotype is just the toolkit that the organisms use for survival and replication. The second question is its opposite: Which parts constitute the essence of life? That is, the way we understand life currently? We could see the organism as the essential unit and the genome as its data storage facility. Because of these differing definitions of synthetic biology, the views on the meaning of life and its very essence demand different views likewise.

According to Benner of the Westheimer Institute for Science and Technology at Gainesville, Florida, there are two apparently opposite definitions of synthetic biology. On the one hand, among engineers, Benner said at the conference SB5.0 held at Stanford University recently, "synthetic biology seeks to use natural parts of biological systems (like DNA fragments or protein biobricks) to create assemblies that do things that are not done by natural biology such as digital computation or manufacturing of specialty chemicals." On the other hand, among chemists, by contrast, "synthetic biology seeks to use unnatural molecular parts to do things that are done by natural biology."

For us to be familiar with how synthetic biology works, we would like to follow each step of the process.

In constructing DNA for synthetic biology, we should recall that DNA means Deoxyribonucleic acid and it is the molecule which makes up the chromosomes. It has a double helix structure which was discovered in 1953 by Watson and Crick, as revealed in the book, The Double Helix (Watson, 1968), building on the work of Rosalind Franklin and Maurice Wilkins. It contains pairs of molecules that fit together and are called "base pairs". The base pairs are: adenine/thymine and guanine/cytosine.

These pairs create a "binary code" that in some sense provides the instructions to create the building blocks for cells or regulate their use. DNA can be replicated by splitting the two strands and creating the opposite strand from raw materials within a cell. For all living creatures and most viruses, DNA contains many of the instructions for life; however, scientists are beginning to understand the process to be more complex than previously thought. Next would be to re-engineer the DNA into recombinant DNA and create the desired DNA cells. The resulting genetically modified organism is called transgenic.

Emerging Benefits and Risks of Synthetic Biology

Because today we have learned to make new sequences of DNA from scratch, thanks to the principles of modern engineering, we are now able to use computers and laboratory chemicals to re-design new organisms that are not found in the natural world. They do new things and they make things possible for us where once they were dubbed impossible. This is the very essence of synthetic biology - its tremendous potential to benefit the world. Scientists are now able to produce better medical drugs, better crops for farmers, and more efficient renewable energy like biofuels and bioluminescent lighting. In fact, we can make trees and plants glow by re-engineering their genetic code.

Some new things that are happening because of synthetic biology are as follows:

Myers (2012) set up "Bio-Design" at the Museum of Modern Art, New York. She describes her artwork as a combination of "Nature, Science, and Creativity." It focuses on the experiments on bio-design in collaboration with scientists that have gained tremendous momentum – giving way to a new form of organic design. As defined, biodesign refers specifically to living organisms as essential components of design, thus the need of design artists to collaborate with biologists and other scientists. One interesting feature that uses the concept of synthetic biology is the biobrick. To produce this biobrick one needs sand,bacteria or microorganism, and a chemical mix of calcium chloride and urea to initiate microbial induced precipitation (MIP), whereby the bacteria and the grains of sand are glued together to form stone. This has its risks, though, because making biobrick can produce toxic ammonia as a by-product. Thus, the challenge is how to contain this potentially dangerous gas and prevent it from spreading in the environment.

Another interesting biodesign is related to our bioluminescent lighting system. In Myers's book, the Bio-Light in the "Microbial Home" is made up of an array of glass cells that can be hung or wall mounted and are connected via silicon tubes at the base of a food reservoir. Illumination is provided either by bioluminescent bacteria – maintained by methane from a bio-digester – or by chemically-charged fluid florescent proteins. Both produce light at low temperatures.

There are a number of risks posed by synthetic biology which we need to look into and these are as follows:

The first risk is posed by the impetus to rush the innovation to the market in the desire to commercialize the new technologies without first looking into all aspects – both benefits and risks – of the innovation. We understand that biotech companies invest large sums of money for the innovation and they need to get a return on their investment, also for their investors. If the project is a government initiative, the more is the desire to recover the investment in the new technology. To address this risk, there is a need to be cautious, to take time before commercialization, in short, not to rush without considering all aspects of the innovation using synthetic biology.

As to government regulations, there are no specific policies and rules related to these emerging synthetic biology-inspired innovations. While there are existing regulations for biotechnology and nanotechnology, there is none for synthetic biology. Hence, there is a need to come up with a Committee to take charge of regulating the new methods and processes of synthetic biology to ensure that the innovations do not pose risks.

Being technology innovators ourselves, we do not wish to cause harm to anyone who will use our GlowGlobe lighting system. We will take precautions and adhere to regulations. However, at this time, there are no clear regulations to follow. We think the regulations should be put in- place as there are a number of us who are into synthetic biology.

Synthetic Biology in the Future

In the next 10 years, synthetic biology will lead to more disruptive innovations that will change many of our traditional ways of doing things. The commercialization of technologies using synthetic biology will bring innovations in medicine, agriculture, and energy. The engineering of microbes to support bioluminescent lighting systems will likewise be a part of these disruptive innovations. Synthetic biologists will then be able to re-engineer complex biological systems with efficacy to emit light.

Dr. Soontorn Piromsartkoon with Prof. Worsak, President of AIT, in Bangkok, Thailand. Photo taken by AIT staff.

CHAPTER 18

Perpetual Light Biotechnologies: The Case of GlowGlobe Startup

The fourth startup company under the nascent global bioluminescent industry is our own Perpetual Light Biotechnologies with its GlowGlobe product. This chapter is devoted to our disruptive innovation on bioluminescent lighting system presented as a business case.

Overview of bioluminescence perpetual lighting

Our idea of developing a perpetual lighting system using bioluminescence was inspired by the light of the fireflies. There is something magical about their glowing light. As children growing up in two different countries, Thailand and the Philippines, we both were fascinated by the glow emitted by fireflies in the dark.

We learned later that there has been 50 years of research on this phenomenon of bioluminescent organisms both in marine and land habitats. Most of the bioluminescent species are found in the ocean, but some are on land like the fireflies, glowworms, the algae. But despite fifty years of scientific research, until now attempts to use the bioluminescent light for commercial purposes have not been successful, and only two startups in the United States, one startup in France, and our own startup in Thailand are bold enough to engage in disruptive innovation by developing bioluminescent lighting systems that mimic the light emitted by fireflies, squids, jellyfish, and other bioluminescent organisms.

In 2016, John Lee wrote a book, titled, *Bioluminescence, the Nature of the Light* (Lee, 2016). It is a very comprehensive book on topic of bioluminescence as it provides a long history of scientific investigation on the phenomenon of bioluminescence.

Lee (2016) pointed out that it was Pliny the Elder (23-79 CE) in his *Naturalis Historia*, who wrote quite detailed descriptions of many bioluminescent animals: glowworms and fireflies, the luminous mollusk *Pholas dactylus* (a Roman delicacy), the purple jellyfish *Pelagia noctilus* common in the Mediterranean, the lantern fish, and the fungi, glowing wood and mushrooms. Until now, these are the very bioluminescent organisms that are the subjects of investigation by researchers worldwide. What makes them emit light naturally? How can we harness this biological source of light to light the world?

Those are the very same questions we raised when we

embarked on this project on developing perpetual lighting system using bioluminescence. As we earlier mentioned, our inspiration came from the light emitted by fireflies. We all know now that fireflies are able to emit light through a chemical reaction in which luciferin is converted to oxyluciferin by the luciferase enzyme. These are the chemicals produced by the fireflies in their bodies. The luciferin (from Lucifer, the Light Bearer) is the key to the emission of light by certain organisms. It needs of course oxygen to combine with for the chemical reaction to take place. The energy released by this chemical reaction is in the form of living light. It might surprise us to know that nearly 19% of the world population is in the dark. And that the worldwide energy consumption is also around 20% on lighting. Thus, we realize that if we can produce lighting system using bioluminescence, we can reduce electricity costs significantly and provide light to those who have no access to electricity and since bioluminescent light does not have carbon footprint, then it will be able to reduce the carbon emissions of fossil fuels and contribute to the mitigation of the adverse effects of global climate change.

In the course of our research on bioluminescence, we found out that the major challenge being faced by our colleagues in the nascent bioluminescent light industry is how to prolong the duration of the bioluminescent light. For the group from MIT, the glowing watercress plant produces light for short duration. For the company in France, the bioluminescent lighting system lasts also for a short time. Hence, we are developing a perpetual lighting system using

Above Photo: Dr. Marites A. Khanser, holding the placard for winning for her team The Best Idea Award from IDE 2018 Accelerator of Thailand and MIT-Boston USA, during the November 26, 2017 first session in Bangkok, Thailand. Photo taken by IDE staff, November 26, 2017, Bangkok, Thailand

bioluminescence. How we can achieve this is therefore our major challenge.

Startup Company Background

When we were selected to join as Fellows of the IDE (Innovation-Driven Entrepreneurship) 2018 Accelerator Program of Thailand and MIT-Boston, USA, from November 26, 2017 to March 21, 2018, we called our team as Team Perpetual Light Biotechnologies. There were four of us in the team that were trained under the IDE Accelerator with mentors and coaches from UTCC in Thailand and MIT in the

USA. We learned the 24 Steps to Disciplined Entrepreneurship and on how to build up our business opportunity. We won the Best Idea Award 2018 for our product idea on perpetual lighting system using bioluminescence. Unlike the other teams in the Accelerator, our product idea belongs to the frontiers of science since we will be using biotechnology, specifically, synthetic biology. To quote Steve Jobs (Issacson, 2011), "The biggest innovation of the twenty-first century will be the intersection of technology and biology. A new era is beginning."

Indeed, the disruptive innovations today and in the foreseeable future are coming and will be coming from the intersection of technology and biology. Biotechnology presents exciting possibilities to make our life better, to secure the world from hunger, disease, and other world woes. From our experience with IDE Accelerator, we decided to put up a startup company called Perpetual Light Biotechnologies and to locate it in Thailand.

Mission and vision and philosophy for the startup

Our trademark for our brand is GlowGlobe Lighting System and our tagline is "Glowing the Globe." We believe that our bioluminescent light is a living light, and it is the Light of the Creator. Thus, when "the Light of the Creator spreads throughout the Globe, darkness and evil will vanish from the face of the Earth."

Our Mission

We want to be an inventor of bioluminescent perpetual lighting to generate alternative light for the 1400 million of the world population that are still in darkness and have no access to electricity.

We want to contribute to environmental protection through our green energy that does not have carbon footprint.

Our Vision

We want to be a leader of green energy in the world though our GlowGlobe product, a perpetual bioluminescent lighting system.

Our Business Philosophy

We believe that creativity and innovation will drive the intersection of technology and biology.

Competitive advantage of our product

Using Porter's Five Competitive Forces Model

In analyzing the global competition in the nascent bioluminescent lighting industry, we would like to apply Porter's Five Competitive Forces Model as follows:

Bargaining power of buyers

In terms of bargaining power of buyers, who are our customers? Do we have a market for our GlowGlobe product? During our IDE interviews with prospective customers in USA, the Philippines, and Thailand, we found out that there are customers who are very interested to see the new product which is reputed to be environmental friendly and to buy the bioluminescent lighting. This provides us the inspiration to proceed with the commercialization of our product. But they want to know the price compared to the current electric lamps and bulbs they use in their households. Price is a factor in the competition. Since in the production of bioluminescent lighting products will initially be prohibitive, the buyers will have to contend with premium prices. But once full commercialization happens, most of the startups will then be offering competitive prices.

Prospective customers of our GlowGlobe products will also look into the duration of bioluminescent light to find out if indeed we can have continuous living light. As of now, we have already found the solution to perpetual lighting but we still need to do experiments and trials to see if we can make it happen. Customers might also look into the safety of using our product.

Bargaining power of suppliers

The next competitive force to reckon with in the global competition of bioluminescent lighting nascent industry (i.e. at the moment, the industry does not exist since there are no commercially available products yet in the market) is the bargaining power of suppliers. The supply chain distribution will have to be established for our product. We may opt to include it in online grocery stores or specialty stores. But there is the problem of physical distribution and the care that our products need so these do not get into the wrong hands. We may have regional distributors or sell through Alibaba for the China market and Toechok for the Thailand market, and of course, the global market since these two stores are online platforms. We may have B2B e-commerce and B2C for individual customers who are curious and daring enough to try novel products.

We also have suppliers of our raw materials needs, i.e. the nutrients we need for the host organisms that emit light, the encasement material, the lighting designs, etc. We need these from laboratories, from gene cells companies, from engineering firms, among others. We can see that it will be a web of global suppliers and they can impose their own requirements. Likewise, we can accept only green suppliers, meaning, they get certifications that they engage in green business. This may be difficult to find since not all companies are into green business, but we believe it will be a good manufacturing practice.

Threat of new entrants

So far as the threat of new entrants is concerned, at the moment, we are all new entrants to an emerging bioluminescent light industry. However, there are still a number of researchers who are into bioluminescence, but it will be no problem for us, since we can form a strategic alliance with these startups.

Once the market for bioluminescent light will be well established, there will surely be new entrants in the industry and so we need to innovate and never to be complacent because new entrants may bring in more competitive products at lesser prices.

Threat of substitute products

In terms of threat of substitute products, there are many lighting systems available in the market. There is the solar panel which harnesses the light from the sun and enables households to reduce their electric consumption significantly. There are other inventions concerning lighting systems we may not be aware of, and might enter the market as substitute for our GlowGlobe products. We need to anticipate the threat that it will pose on our competitiveness in the market. Substitute products might offer lower prices compared to our product. Of course, we cannot fully compete with electric lighting systems because our products are "cold light", meaning it does not emit thermal heat.

Rivalry among firms

In previous chapters of this book, we introduce some of those companies that are into developing bioluminescent light for possible use as an alternative source of light. However at this time, no company in the world has commercialized this bioluminescent light on a large scale.

We believe that the rivalry of firms will come from companies manufacturing solar panels, or engaged in biomass for commercial use, and those companies which are into wind mills projects.

Solar panels are currently available and companies selling solar panels offer an alternative energy to compete with electric companies. These companies will be our competitors in the future.

Biomass being manufactured by companies for commercial use will also pose a threat to our GlowGlobe product since it is a renewable energy also. We will take note of the competition in this area.

Lastly, we will consider wind mills as our competitors. Companies engaged in wind mills projects will be able to supply electricity to some communities but not enough to supply other far communities.

Our company mission is to let the world know that the phenomenon of bioluminescence has a commercial potential. Making use of the bioluminescent light as alternative lighting system is for us a noble mission. We realize that it may take ten years for the disruptive innovation we call perpetual lighting system using bioluminescence for it to become accepted as an alternative light globally. Because it is green energy, it will have a good impact on the goal of environmental protection; it will help reduce carbon emissions since bioluminescent light does not have carbon footprint. If many people in the world will be using our GlowGlobe products, they will be contributing to saving our Planet Earth from global warming. In times of natural disasters, the bioluminescent light will still provide light even when electric posts will have been destroyed by hurricanes or typhoons. Should electricity fail in a future world where our cities will be under water because of the rising sea level and glacier melting, our great, great grandchildren will still have a living light to illuminate their world.

An imagined molecular biology laboratory where the GlowGlobe perpetual bioluminescent light is being developed as a prototype.

An imagined office being lighted by the GlowGlobe perpetual bioluminescent light as ceiling bio lamps.

How Bioluminescent Light Will Benefit The World

CHAPTER 19

Benefits of Using Bioluminescent Lighting System

Comparative Advantage of using our

Bioluminescent Lighting system

We have come to this part of our book where we present the benefits of using the bioluminescent lighting system. We would like to highlight the comparative advantage of using our GlowGlobe product when it will be available in the market. This chapter identifies the various benefits that customers will get from using our product.

The comparative advantages we would like to bring to your attention are on the following: advantage over electric lighting; pros and cons of using our product; the need to use bioluminescent light, or the benefits that the product brings to the user; the benefits from the natural world and the cost savings that will be derived by using the GlowGlobe products over a long term.

Existing electric lighting system vs. bioluminescent lighting

At present, we rely heavily on electric lighting to illuminate our homes, our workplaces, and our streets and avenues. Our electricity costs are part of the burden we carry since we need to light our homes and offices. In far flung areas like rural villages, the people have no access to electricity so they have to make do with kerosene lamps, while 19% of the world population live in darkness. Since electric utility companies are usually monopolies, they can have the power to dictate the price of electric power so our electric bills tend to increase as we increase our electric consumption. If there is an alternative lighting like our bioluminescent lighting system, then the people will have an option to go for it rather than continue using electric light.

Advantages and Disadvantages of using Bioluminescent Lighting system

Let us try to evaluate the advantages and disadvantages of using bioluminescent lighting system once it is already available in the market.

The advantages are as follows:

Price. When mass production takes place, the price of the bioluminescent light product will become cheaper.

Product. The GlowGlobe product will be designed as a living light, hence, perpetual light lasts for as long as the host is alive and maintained.

Place of Distribution. Once the products become available, then a supply chain of distribution will take place. Although there will be distributors the products can also be purchased online.

Promotion. The bioluminescent light will be promoted worldwide and this will enable the product to be on top of the customers' mind to the customers.

There are certain disadvantages in the use of the bioluminescent light, and these are:

Price. This will be premium at the early stage of the commercialization of the product and only those who are into alternative lifestyle might be able to afford the price.

Product. The bioluminescent light products will need some vigilance on the part of the buyers to ensure that the product will still continue to be useful as light. This type of product is produced through the process of synthetic biology and might prove risky if the user will not be vigilant. We will see to it that there will be instructions for the proper use of the product.

Place of Distribution. The bioluminescent light products may not be very accessible to all those who want to buy them since in the early stage of commercialization, the products will be limited. However, ten years from now, they will just be an ordinary alternative lighting system for all.

Promotion. There will be heavy advertising and promotions that will take place to introduce the bioluminescent light products to the market and this will also have an impact on the price.

Why do we need Bioluminescent Lighting system?

Here are some important reasons why we need bioluminescent lighting system:

Benefits of the natural world (environmental protection)

We are harnessing the light of bioluminescent organisms like the fireflies as an alternative source of light. For millions of years, the bioluminescent organisms have emitted light naturally and yet we have not fully made use of this phenomenon for human purposes. Mimicking the manner these organisms produce living light which will benefit mankind in the years to come because the products will be more resilient in times of natural disasters.

Substitute for 1400 million of world population who have no access to lighting supply

Our mission is to offer an alternative source of light for the 1400 million of the world who have no access to electricity and other alternative source of light. This is too big a market that our company will have to supply. However, the competitors will also be supplying this untapped market, so prospects are good for alternative sources of lighting system.

Alternative of renewable energy

Since bioluminescent light is green energy, it is an alternative for such renewable energy as solar panel. Customers can choose bioluminescent lighting products over solar panel, depending on the price and ease of use.

Cost Saving for Users

Over the long term, we expect that there will be cost savings for the users of our bioluminescent light product which need not be replaced too often. There will thus be no bills to pay for using it, unlike in the case of electric lighting. The cost of replacement will be greatly reduced.

CHAPTER 20

Environmental and Health Protection

Introduction

Our concern for environmental protection has been presented in previous chapters of this book. We note that due to global climate change, our Planet Earth is being affected adversely by grim scenarios of natural disasters causing destructions to humans, plants and animals and all inhabitants of the planet. Companies have to be concerned about the impact of their business activities on the environment and should take part in its protection as their corporate social responsibility.

Why are we devoting a chapter on environmental protection as well as health protection? What has this got to do with our disruptive innovation, our bioluminescent perpetual lighting system? We would like to believe that bioluminescent light is environment-friendly. We would like to use the concept of environmental impact assessment and health as an international tool to assess the extent of the compliance of companies, including our own startup, to the tenets of environmental and health protection.

Environmental Impact Assessment and Health

We have found an assessment tool that can help us assess the environmental and health impact of bioluminescent lighting system. The Environmental Impact Assessment (EIA) is the "evaluation of the effects likely to arise from a major project significantly affecting the environment." (Jay et al, 2007). This is a systematic process for assessing the likely environmental consequences of a project or action. This is meant to ensure that if the project is approved it will be not contribute to health problems and environmental degradation.

The EIA seeks a balanced approach to manage the risks related to a project. Its guiding principles are **clarity** and **certainty** both in management of **costs** and the avoidance the risk of challenge. Let us look at each of these as follows:

Clarity. While the proponents may not always know the potential health and environmental risks nor have they the expertise to do so, nevertheless, they have the information that will guide the public health professionals and environmental officers to assess the potential risks of a project which can contribute to the EIA or to help in identifying potential mitigation measures.

Certainty. This pertains to early engagement with developers or project owners and consultees who are able to offer mutual benefits and a shared understanding of the degree of certainty. This is so since late engagement may bring in surprises and might prove costly to the project proponents. Early engagement avoids this situation.

Costs. Projects should be run on timetables and with strict budgets since delays will mean additional costs. The EIA must focus on assessments that most likely will have significant effects. For example, planning that involves stakeholders should be made as efficiently as possible.

Challenge. This pertains to the need to be legally compliant and to have the risks of the project properly identified and managed. Early engagement with health professionals and environmental experts need to be done so as to avoid challenges that might delay the approval and implementation of the project. The challenges may come from unforeseen risks, higher costs due to additional requirements and legal challenges.

The above are the principles that will guide us in assessing whether the bioluminescent lighting system if it can comply with the four Cs.

Importance of health and environmental assessment

Given the four principles of EIA, we would like to know if the new innovations on lighting system using bioluminescence can comply with these guidelines. This involves not only our own GlowGlobe perpetual lighting system using bioluminescence but also our colleagues in the industry working on similar but not identical disruptive innovations.

When we say clarity, what we need to look into this requirement is the process of synthetic biology that enables the bioluminescent light to be produced as lighting products. Is the process clear and are we transparent about the process? Is the protocol followed strictly by our scientists who are in charge in the laboratory? Are the health professionals provided with adequate information regarding unwarranted health risks like pandemic or some other forms of illness through the mutation of the microbes that are used as hosts?

As of today, there are still no clear government regulations for our innovative biotechnology since there is still no full scale commercialization of bioluminescent lighting products available in the world market. In terms of environmental protection, are all startup companies aware of the potential environmental hazards in the use of bioluminescent light as commercial products? And if there are, have these been identified and have mitigation measures been planned?

As disruptive innovations, bioluminescent lighting products are indeed so pioneering that they will disrupt current regulations and controls such as EIA and other regulatory international bodies.

When it comes to certainty, we need to have consultations with countries where we want to market our products. There are regulations in the United States such as EIA, but there are other regulating agencies that we have already identified in the previous chapters of this book. We need to comply with their requirements and be certain that nothing has been left to chance.

In terms of costs, since we are offering a new innovation, disruptive at that, to the customers for the first time, we anticipate that it will be costly for us in the early stage of business development, while we are producing our prototype,but also in the further phase of product development until its commercialization. But if early in the product development stage we already anticipate some of the challenges we will encounter in the future, we can then prepare for them and avoid some surprises in the later stages.

Lastly, we are hoping that there will be less challenges along the way of commercialization and the marketing of our perpetual bioluminescent lighting system. The manner to ensure that depends on how we will avoid major challenges in terms of market acceptance and regulatory issues through adequate and accurate anticipation, prediction, planning, and preparation.

Bioluminescent Perpetual Lighting System is Environmental - Friendly

We are confident that our bioluminescent lighting system will be environmental- friendly. This is because it is a product of living light which will create no carbon footprint. In fact, as an alternative light, it will reduce carbon footprint; its production will not cause carbon emissions nor will it have fossil fuels.

We will also ensure that the environment will not be

affected by our product when it reaches its shelf life because we intend the light to be continuous for as long as the host is alive. We can likewise recycle it for the users and return to them, at a minimal fee, a renewed and recycled bioluminescent light lamp or light material.

Bioluminescent Perpetual Lighting System is the new alternative of green energy

Finally, another benefit of using bioluminescent lighting system such as our GlowGlobe product is its being an alternative of green energy. We do have renewable energy currently in the market. We have solar panels, we have biomass, we have windmills, among others. Now, our product will be an alternative green energy since it does not harm the environment and is a renewable and even a perpetual living light. We will discuss more details of its benefits in the next chapter.

CHAPTER 21

Alternative Green Energy

Introduction: our bioluminescent perpetual light

Our bioluminescent perpetual lighting system will be the first in the world since it offers a unique product proposition: It has a perpetual living light that provides illumination to homes, offices, malls, and streets as well as avenues. In addition, since it has a biological source for its lighting it does not contribute to carbon emissions and therefore, it can be considered as green energy. We would like to offer our product as an alternative energy. Of course, once commercialized, our GlowGlobe perpetual lighting system will have to compete with other existing models of renewable energy. We now look into the competition for comparison purposes.

Comparison of Existing Models of Renewable Energy

There are existing models of renewable energy and we understand that this situation accounts for the competition. For instance, solar panel is considered a renewable energy. It harnesses the rays from the sun and for as long as there is sunshine, it can provide light by converting the sun's rays into electricity. When we install solar panels in our homes, these will help in getting rid of harmful greenhouse gas emissions, thus so reducing global warming. However, what is the disadvantage of using solar panels? We need to install them outdoors as they need sunlight to get charged and so they are quite expensive. So, price is a factor we need to consider for our GlowGlobe product; it should be affordable.

When we were in Crete, Greece, we saw hundreds of windmills generating electricity through wind power. We were told that these were modern turbines that produce electricity for the olive orchards and other farmlands in Crete, Greece. Indeed, windmills as we know them now are usually located in large agricultural areas where there are large plots of land. They have also to be located in areas where it is windy to harness the power of the wind. Wind power is a renewable energy since it does not bring any harmful waste to people and the environment. Thus, it qualifies as green energy. However, where wind is not available, one must discover ways to store the electricity that these windmills produced.

In comparison, the product, our bioluminescent perpetual lighting system, is also an alternative green energy which does not emit thermal heat, rather, it emits what we call "cold light." Thus, it cannot be used in the same manner that we use wind power to generate heat and electricity as a source of electric power. The uses of our products will be for lighting purposes, such as bioluminescent lamps and lighting materials for the homes, offices, and malls as well as for lighting up streets and avenues.

Another renewable energy is the use of biomass. This has something to do with recycled waste from landfills and biofuel is the result. This is also green energy since the biofuels do not have greenhouse gas emissions and provide alternative energy for us. The question is if they are less expensive than solar panels and whether they are widely available in the market. People still use electricity from power utilities and have electric consumption as a part of their expense. Of course, when solar panels and biomass are combined, there will be less electricity consumption.

While our perpetual bioluminescent lighting system offers an alternative model for renewable energy, we will compete in a different way. We will have a different market segment and we will target green customers; that is, customers who are consciously buying only green products as an alternative lifestyle. These are buyers who are conscious of the effects of certain products on the environment and will patronize those only products that contribute to environmental protection.

Competitive Advantage of
Bioluminescent Perpetual Lighting System

We do believe that we have a competitive advantage

when we consider the competition ahead of us. When we think of disruptive innovation, we will use the product innovation model and then assess our chances of success.

In terms of price, we will see to it that the price of our products will be affordable so many customers can buy. Solar panels as we learned earlier are quite costly to invest in and they are subject to depreciation. Windmills are difficult to set up and need a lot of investment and a lot of land space. Biomass projects need the government or NGOs since they are huge projects and again needs large investment to set up. Affordability is indeed an issue.

Conclusion

Having assessed the competition for our perpetual bioluminescent lighting system, we realize that we can ably compete in the nascent bioluminescent lighting industry. As of today, there is still no competition at all since not one of the startups has reached full commercialization of their bioluminescent lighting products. But it will not take long for these products to be available in the global market. Our goal is to be a first mover because we believe that we have the best solution in this area for a disruptive innovation in the future, at least until 2050. We will also be responding to the needs of Industry 4.0 by offering a product that makes use of the concepts of biotechnology and synthetic biology. We are confident that we will be able to achieve our mission, vision and goals for the Perpetual Light Biotechnologies.

CHAPTER 22

Solution to Reducing Carbon Footprint

Introduction

In previous chapters, we devote much of the discussion on reducing carbon footprint through human activities. We recently conducted a study (Khanser and Racaza, 2016) on measuring the carbon trading and footprint of selected companies in South East Asia through a research grant awarded by the London-based CIMA (Chartered Institute of Management Accountants). Our findings showed that there are companies that have followed the green path; meaning, they engage in green business and have succeeded in contributing to the reduction of carbon footprint in their manufacturing operations. One of the ways to reduce carbon footprint is to adopt renewable energy in their own companies. Some of the companies that are able to earn carbon emission credits which they can use to trade in voluntary offset market. In this instance, they engage in carbon trading. Thus, it is a good manufacturing practice to engage in green business.

In the case of our perpetual bioluminescent lighting system, our startup will also be considered engaging in green business with the goal of providing affordable alternative green energy. Thus, we will be offering a solution to carbon footprint reduction.

Carbon Footprint Reduction:
How it Works through Bioluminescent Light

One question that must be uppermost in our minds is this: How can the use of bioluminescent lighting products help in reducing carbon footprint?

If we consider bioluminescence as a living light produced naturally by light emitting organisms, then we can reasonably say that there is no carbon footprint at all. However, once the bioluminescent light is harnessed for the lighting system of humans, then we can begin to ask such question as, whether the process of production of the biological source of light will produce greenhouse gas emissions or have carbon emission which will contribute to global warming.

Using the Product Life Cycle Analysis, we can trace the carbon footprint in the manufacturing of a product from the start of the process until the product reaches the end users. The bioluminescent light will be produced in a laboratory, then will go into engineering design, then it will go through packaging, until it will be distributed through a supply chain, and ultimately reaches the customers or end users. Along this path, carbon emissions may have happened.

One thing we are sure of, our perpetual bioluminescent lighting system is environmental-friendly and does not contribute to carbon footprint. This is so because it has a biological source and does not emit carbon dioxide.

Minimizing Carbon Footprint in the Future

Indeed, there is an urgent need for inventions and innovations that will have to address the problem of global warming, and in general global climate change. One solution that we offer for the future is our disruptive innovation: the GlowGlobe product. It is our noble goal to contribute significantly to saving the planet Earth from destruction and the preservation of the human race.

PART SIX

Inventions For The Next 50 Years

CHAPTER 23

Ideas That Have Not Yet Been Imagined

Ideas are Everywhere

We have come to the last part of our book where we intend to give some helpful tips on generating business ideas and present some possible inventions for the next 50 years and even beyond until Year 2100. We would like to share our experience of being able to think of a product idea that belongs to the frontiers of science. We had so much imagination that when we saw the fireflies, we imagined a lighting system using bioluminescence. We discovered during our research that the history of bioluminescence research now spans for 50 years. In the next ten years, our GlowGlobe product will just be an ordinary lighting system that will provide light to the world. It was an idea borne of our imaginative minds, and here we now are, we are about to launch such a living light much like the light of fireflies.

We consider ourselves as idea generators, meaning, we think of many ideas sometimes twenty years or fifty years ahead of our time. But no matter. We believe that the future has already arrived in some parts of the world and we resonate with this future, but it has not necessarily arrived in our respective countries, i.e. Thailand and the Philippines. We echo the challenge of Fredrick Haren (2004) "What can you think of that has not yet been imagined?"

Indeed, in the next fifty years, what product ideas can we think of that have not yet been imagined?

The product ideas that we would like to share with you are those that will attempt to provide solutions to the emerging and pressing world problems, issues, and challenges, particularly, on environment and climate change, health, green business, and machine learning, as well as Science and Technology-driven issues like artificial intelligence (AI) and Internet of Things (IoT), biotechnology, synthetic biology, space exploration, solar power in space, nanotechnology, wealth creation, and the future of humanity.

Ideas that have not yet been imagined

We love to quote Einstein about his belief on the power of imagination. He believed that imagination is more important than knowledge. Indeed, imagination enables us to go beyond knowledge, to explore realms that belong to the world of the very small or of the vast and large expanse of multiverses. Before Einstein arrived at the theory of relativity, he first imagined 30 different worlds, as captured in the book of Lightman (1993) *Einstein's Dreams*. Thus, we must develop our imagination in order that we can come up with product ideas that have never been imagined.

Take for instance the concept of teleportation. The idea that we can transport material things by using our minds from point A to point B is still considered in the realm of science fiction. However, if such can be made possible, then we will no longer need freight couriers since our minds can just teleport materials from one place to the other. Teleportation can also be useful in space travel. Perhaps, humans who will colonize Mars need to be "teleported", i.e. de-materialized because the situation in outer space may be too harsh and brutal for humans to endure physically-immense distance from Earth in light years, extreme temperatures, and other adverse conditions we find hard to imagine. Teleportation is the power of mind over matter. Elon Musk is the pioneer on space exploration and the colonization of Mars by humans. It is just a matter of time before Musk will be able to bring humans to Mars.

Another idea that had been considered by Nikola Tesla, the greatest world inventor, is the harnessing of electric power from the skies. At that time, he was ridiculed, mocked, laughed at for such a crazy idea of the solar power from space. True, he was not able to invent the machine to harness such solar power up in the sky. However, there are attempts today, according to Kaku (2011) to harness such an energy from the sky. If that happens, our GlowGlobe products will have a stiff competition. The idea is called space solar power (SSP). This is energy production coming from outer space through satellite collectors. This is such a wild idea, we might say, but we look hard again, and chances are that we will see how great is the possibility for it to be invented.

Though a magnificent idea, the major challenge is the prohibitive cost of manufacturing many satellites to be sent in space above the earth to collect the energy from the sun and beam it to the Earth in the form of microwave radiation. We believe this is an idea worth pursuing in the near future. Thus, can our imagination visualize such a product idea? This is very similar to what Tesla wanted to do although his concept was to harness electric power for free from lightning. It was of course an idea that may look too dangerous to consider but solar space power is actually a very good idea.

In 2009, the Japanese Trade Ministry announced a plan to investigate a space power satellite system (Kaku, 2011: 253). They were looking at Mitsubishi Electric and other Japanese companies to join together in the program that was worth $10 billion. The idea is to launch a solar power station in space and to generate a billion watts of electric power. This is a huge project and we will wait for further developments along this area.

We believe that it will be an alternative form of energy from the space although it sounds like science fiction to many of us today. As authors of this book on a disruptive innovation from light emitting organisms, we are not surprised that such an idea is now being pursued. It is just a matter of time before such solar space station will be installed and the solar space satellites will become a reality.

Imagination is the Key to discover New ideas

We conclude that it is indeed the power of imagination that will enable us to discover new ideas that have never been yet heard of today. For world famous author J.K. Rowling the importance of the imagination should be recognized by our young generation and should be encouraged by us, their elders. Because of her imagination, world famous author Rowling created the entirely imagined colorful world of Harry Potter and in the process, wrote books that brought her worldwide fame and fortune. Her book, *Very Good Lives: The Fringe Benefits of Failure and the Importance of Imagination* (Rowling, 2008) should be read by our young people so they will appreciate the value of failure and the power of imagination.

Yes, a word of caution, though. The fringe benefits of failure are pointed out by Rowling (2008). In imagining ideas that are beyond the minds of ordinary mortals, the inventor is bound to fail many times, in fact, failure would constitute 90% of every successful invention. Likewise, we have to be prepared to be mocked at, laughed at, ridiculed and be called crazy because of our ideas that have never been imagined by the ordinary citizens of the world. We, inventors and innovators, are risk takers and are not afraid of failure because to imagine worlds that are beyond the current understanding of what a world should be, demands a capacity to accept failure and still to dare to dream and to imagine.

Imagination is the key to bring us to a world where humanity will evolve as spiritual beings that are far superior to robots or artificial intelligence. Our leaps of imagination are what differentiate us from the robots that will soon dominate our future world, until 2025 according to Industry 4.0 where artificial intelligence will surpass human intelligence in many areas except the HUMAN IMAGINATION.

CHAPTER 24

Some Inventions of the Future

"We do not need magic to transform our world; we carry all the power we need inside ourselves already."- J.K. Rowling (2008).

Inventions for the Taking

We would like to encourage the young people to be more creative, imaginative, and innovative by including this bonus chapter for our readers. We would like to explore possible inventions for the future, for the next 50 years, at least, but we can go beyond that until 2100, for the next century.

There is a book by Michio Kaku (2011) our favorite physicist, *Physics of the Future: The Inventions that will Transform our Lives*. It is a treasure trove of inventions for the next 100 years. The good thing about Kaku (2011) is that he interviewed numerous scientists and inventors that enabled him to predict what inventions are possible. In particular, he identifies what technologies will mature in the next 100 years and he said will ultimately determine the fate of humanity.

Technologies that will Change the Future

There are a number of innovations and discoveries that will change the landscape for the next century. The areas that we can identify include the economic, political, and social aspects of our lives. There will be many challenges and opportunities that will present themselves to us because of the new technologies that will mature by 2100. The inventions we would like you to consider will be in some areas only and we can only hope to give you a number of inventions for the future, some of which may appear like science fiction for you; however based on our observations, most of the technologies we have today were actually stuff of science fiction just 50 years ago.

Let us look at the future of the computers. Kaku (2011) calls it "mind over matter." The power of computers affects the way we communicate with the rest of the world through the Internet. In 50 years, so many technological advances in computing and on how we will access the Internet will render our current laptops and smart phones obsolete. There are many inventions we can think of, especially connected with information technology, which will change the way we think of computers linking us to the Internet.

Let us think of inventions where we need not bring our laptops and smartphones with us. One invention that Kaku (2011) pointed out is the use of Internet contact lenses that will serve as our computer. Can we imagine such a replacement to our beloved iPads, laptops, and iPhones? This kind of invention will enable us to go to the airport without the need to bring personal computers with us. All we need to do is wear our Internet contact lenses that have a chip and LCD display and presto, we will be connected virtually in cyberspace. What other inventions that are related to telecommunications and cyberspace lifestyle can we develop in the future?

1. An invention to keep the Internet contact lenses updated;

2. A mode of payment for this gadget and the manner of its distribution

3. After sales service if the contact lenses will need repair or adjustments

4. All other possible allied services that can be developed to cater to such a change of Internet access.

Let us pause and think; this might randomly give us around ten more inventions we have never imagined before.

5. When the owner of the contact lenses loses it, how is it for him to recover it?

6. How can we become cybertourists by just using our contact lenses, what possible inventions can be made to make our life as tourists in cyberspace comfortable and exciting? We do not need to go to other countries physically to enjoy the tourists sites. What will happen to our current way of managing tourism?

7. As cybershoppers, what inventions can we develop to enable virtual shopping possible using our Internet contact lenses?

8. What innovations can be made to make cybershopping hassle-free, 24/7, and what new modes of delivery of the goods can be designed? (Perhaps, teleportation can solve this problem of delivery of goods ordered from the Internet).

9. As cyberstudents, how will schools respond to this new type of students who will take courses purely online, anywhere, anytime? How will open universities look like? What will happen when there will be no students in the physical classrooms as we know today? What innovations can be developed in the area of electronic learning or cyberlearning when it will become the new normal for students?

10. As cyberemployees or workers, what will happen to physical offices as we know today when employees are virtual and need not report to their workplaces but just log in to their cyber-office and work anywhere, anytime?

As we can see, from just one major disruptive innovation like the Internet contact lenses, so many other inventions will arise to challenge the way we think of accessing and using the Internet. By using our imagination, we can invent many things in the next 50 years.

Biotechnology of the Future

Biotechnology is where our invention, perpetual lighting system using bioluminescence, belongs. What we are proposing to do is to transform the microorganisms to emit light when it is not their nature to do so. By genetically modifying our hosts for the bioluminescent lighting products, we have transformed the lives of some microbes into something else. This is the power of biotechnology and synthetic biology. The downside is that the microbes might also resist their modified nature.

According to Kaku (2011), with the power of biotechnology, we will create perfect bodies, and extend lifespans, short of being immortal. One of the books that we find interesting is *The Songs of the Earth* (Nissenson, 2001). This is a futuristic novel set in Year 2050 (this is not so remote from today, which is 2018, and so just 32 years into the future). In such a future, biotechnology is at its height. Imagine the world of 2050. Most of the major cities in the United States and other parts of the world near the Antarctica or where glaciers have melted, are submerged in water. Cities have become submerged in water environment. Yet, people of this future are able to navigate a watery world because of biotechnology and synthetic biology.

Our bioluminescent light 32 years from now will be the source of light for this submerged world. In the novel, *The Songs of the Earth* (Nissenson, 2001), couples can order the genes they want for their future babies. If the mother likes a son to have the artistic abilities of Picasso, this can be done. Genetic engineering will make this possible. Genius gene cells are up for sale. However, it may turn out that as the genetically engineered artist son as he grows up will resist his talents as an artistic genius. This is the way we see our glowing trees and plants that are bioluminescent. They might resist to be "glowing" trees because in their ancient memory, they could remember that it was not their nature to "glow." Such is the downside of biotechnology and synthetic biology.

Still with the power of biotechnology, we will be able to create life forms that Kaku (2011) said, "have never walked the surface of the earth." We can think of many disruptive innovations that will affect the natural world as we know it today. We can just contemplate what these new life forms will be and we hope that they will be for the betterment of the human race.

If we imagine a submerged world by 2050, there will be many inventions that can be imagined and developed and also disruptive innovations. Some of these will be in the following areas:

11. Watermobiles or water taxis will navigate the watery environment.

12. There will be new designs for houses, some of which may look like aquariums, in a grand style. So we need the imagination of architects and engineers for these disruptive designs.

13. Food may be in the form of pills that can be bought from a store since there might be difficulty in raising farms when the world is submerged in water. So culinary arts should be able to respond to this need for food in powdered form and can be put into pills. There will be no more need for eating as we know it today. People will not be bothered by having dinners, cooking, grocery shopping, etc. Most of the joys of current living may no longer be the way to go.

14. Thus, what inventions are possible for all the activities of nourishing the body when the humans of the

future can have perfect bodies with no place for illnesses and diseases in the world? What will happen to hospitals and clinics? And doctors? We try to imagine all these needs as we know them today. But for all we know, all of our activities today will be non-existent. We can think of around 20major inventions to think about to prepare for a future that is so alien to us today when we are still able to enjoy the Planet Earth's flora and fauna, the four seasons, the beauty of natural environment, and the magnificence of the stars in the skies. In the watery world of the future, we may not see the skies anymore.

For the last chapter of this book, we will contemplate the trajectory of the human race. We will look at technology as a great enabler in the service of humanity. We present our optimism for the future of humanity, despite the fast development in the areas of Artificial Intelligence, Machine Learning, Internet of Things (IoT), nanotechnology, biotechnology, space explorations, synthetic biology, super computing, and the search for aliens in the galaxies.

CHAPTER 25

Technology in the service of human spiritual evolution

Introduction

There is a book that provides us a vision of the future of humanity when we will all have been highly evolved humans. The book is *The Secret of Shambala: In Search of the Eleventh Insight* (Redfield, 1999), one of those New Age books which very imaginatively predict the spiritual evolution of humans. In the book, highly evolved humans on the mystical mountain of Tibet have achieved the highest level of the power of the mind over matter. Teleportation is the ordinary way they bring materials from one point to another by using their mind. They manufacture all they need with the use of mental power; they create invisible doors in their homes that open and close by sheer cognitive suggestions. The inventions we have today with our technology is very crude when compared with the kinds of inventions these highly evolved humans are capable of inventing. We have so much to learn from them. Technology has been instrumental in their spiritual evolution.

We might say that the people of Shambala are just a product of the imagination of the author, James Redfield, but it is very likely to happen in the next 100 years of human existence. At the fast rate we are progressing in advances in science and technology, we can predict we will be able to reach such a high level of human existence.

The Role of Technology in Spiritual Evolution

So, what is the role of technology in human spiritual evolution? We resonate with the query of Vern Barnett, in the article, The Role of Technology in Spiritual Evolution (Brumet, 2011), which is "What effect will developing technology have on spirituality in the future?" His query was answered by Robert Brumet who responded in the book, titled, *Birthing a Great Reality* (Brumet, 2010). In this book, he describes how people can participate in the spiritual evolution of humanity and what role technology might play in it.

Interestingly, Brumet replied that from the perspective of the evolution of human consciousness, saying that "technology can be seen as both an effect and a change agent." (Brumet, 2010). He remarked that the effect of technology parallels that of biological evolution.

Effect of Technology on Human Consciousness

The effect of technology on our human consciousness, according to Brumet, demands a certain level of sophistication of our thought. For instance,the people of Shambala, who have evolved the highest level of thought, were able to make this possible through the different energy levels they cultivated in themselves. At the lowest level, they nourish their physical bodies with food that are largely vegan with raw food and absolutely no dead meat. They believe that dead meat decays in the body and attracts microbes and bacteria; a decomposing body is a signal for these microbes and bacteria to attack, causing illnesses and diseases to us. Of course, the people of Shambala do not also want to kill animals for food, because for them, not eating animal food tends to increase one's energy field.

Then they require that we should have only positive thoughts and never entertain negativities or negative thoughts because these attract negative forces in the universe. With positive thoughts, we attract light, beauty, truth, love, kindness, generosity, compassion, and all those wonderful feelings that make our lives meaningful. Thus, if we want technology to have a positive effect on our human consciousness, we need to be able to entertain positive thoughts such that technology can improve our lives.

Brumet (2010) said that to develop a particular technology, we need to build on previous thoughts about such a technology. We need to build on the levels of sophistication of our thoughts gained through what we have learned in the past until today. The kind of technology that will be invented will correspond to the current situation of the world and the current needs of humanity. For our invention on bioluminescent lighting system, for instance, we build on the past 50 years of scientific research on the phenomenon of bioluminescence. There is the pressing need today to explore other types of renewable energy and in particular, green energy to mitigate the adverse effects of global climate change.

Technology runs parallel to biological evolution since for the latter, life started on Earth with microbes, then through evolution, plants, animals, and humans came to dominate the Planet, and all of these inhabitants of the Earth have evolved as a part of the survival of the fittest as noted by Charles Darwin in his seminal book, *The Origin of Species* (Darwin, 1859).

Depending on the level of technological development that we have achieved so far, the effect of technology will differ and vary in line with our human consciousness.

Technology as Change Agent

Technology has assumed an important role as a change agent in the evolution of humanity. In particular, two important technologies have shaped our human thinking in the Twentieth and Twenty-First Centuries. These two technologies, which have changed the human consciousness in ways that we have not imagined are 1.) the television, and 2) the Internet.

For the television, this was considered a wonderful

invention that it enabled us to acquire information, watch movies, and get news from the world; we could not live without the television before the onset of the Internet. The television brought the world into our own homes which was not possible before.

The Internet has become the most powerful technology ever invented. Today, we cannot imagine a day without access to the Internet. It has tremendously changed the way we live and the manner we communicate, and more importantly, the way we think. According to Brumet, echoing McLuhan, "the medium has become the message." The Internet has a great impact on how our mind functions. The future of humanity will very much revolve on how the Internet will enable technological advancement as never before imagined. In the previous chapter, of this book, we provide scenarios of the future with the Internet as a major change agent.

Changes are happening because of the Internet. Our private life has been invaded and we seem to have lost our privacy; we have no more personal life. In the Facebook, for instance, everybody sees us and knows what we are doing. Our private affairs are for everybody to see and hear, eavesdrop, and participate in. What happened to our personal domain, our personal space? Privacy has lost its power; in cyberspace, we are invaded. We have, indeed become very vulnerable in ways we have never contemplated to happen. Our very thoughts are greatly influenced by the Internet. There is no censorship. Our secrecy and our personal safety are threatened in ways we have never imagined, and this has affected our lives tremendously. We can upload all our thoughts on the Internet and who will edit our ideas, opinions, and our emotions? There are many who have assumed a "cyber personality" or a virtual identity. And the risk it poses is that the individual may no longer be able to distinguish his real personality from that of his virtual identity. The distinction is increasingly getting blurred.

The Big Data about us which are being shared by the social media like Facebook, and Twitter, among others, are being routinely analyzed and packaged for sale to companies who need those Big Data Analytics for their own purposes. We have willingly given information about ourselves and our lives to the Internet whose owners are making big money out of the trillions of information being generated every second, every minute, every hour, say, in Facebook.

We can see that technology has provided us tremendous advantages over our ancestors of the past. Information has become the number one asset, no longer land, physical infrastructure, or buildings, etc. Companies are moving on to digital platforms and conducting business online. Alibaba of Jack Ma has become the biggest and largest e-retailer of the world, because ten years ago, he predicted that the Internet will improve exponentially and that more and more of the Chinese customers will be purchasing online. The vastness of China has been reduced to an Internet-driven supermall.

Thus, technology has become a change agent and has greatly influenced the development of human consciousness. Technology and biological evolution will continue to be "intrinsically woven together", according to Brumet, and that this will continue for an unforeseeable future.

The Soul in Business

How can we save us from ourselves, in the face of the influence of technology, like the Internet, in our lives? What will happen to the human spirit that honors the person and the soul? What will happen to human spirituality?

A solution that is happening today comes from business and industry, a surprising place to find spirituality because for most businesses, profit is the bottomline. And yet, more and more corporate leaders in the world have started to realize that welcoming the human soul and human development makes good business sense (Eilertsen, 2017). In this article of Eilertsen, it focuses on bringing the human spirit to business leadership. He emphasizes that the quest of individuals to develop themselves and others and to bring this aspiration to the workplace makes good business sense.

What the soul in business equates with how corporate leadership brings in the whole person including the human soul into the business and the workplace. However, this has to be made from the soul of religion since ours pertains to the individual and collective experience which recognizes that the human soul should indeed be brought to the workplace. In the past, we call this "workplace spirituality" or "spirituality in the workplace." In essence, this has all to do with the quest of individuals for nourishment not only of their physical bodies but also of the human spirit.

When business takes up the cause of human spiritual evolution, then we need not worry over the impact of technology in our lives. Nowadays, businesses have adopted the triple bottom line consisting of people, planet, and profit. With the soul in business, people as employees and workers are provided with the means for the human development that will enable them to evolve into spiritual beings. Ultimately, we will evolve into higher spiritual beings like the people of the mythical Shambala whose concern for humanity's development occupies their waking hours. Thus, to save humanity is their noble goal.

As technology innovators, we, as authors of this book, would also like to participate in this task of saving humanity and in furthering the human spiritual evolution.

EPILOGUE

As I had been a part of IDE 2018 Accelerator in Thailand, I am so proud that Dr. Khanser and Dr. Soontorn have never given up on this perpetual bioluminescent light project. They both are looking forward to achieving their goal for the project and I am very confident of their success. In the meantime, I understand that they are both engaged in extensive research to develop a workable prototype, while at the same time writing this book to let the readers of the world know that it is possible to have a new alternative green energy.

I am very excited to write this Epilogue for this book because I know both of them have a lot of experience and have in fact taken up environmental advocacy. The book contains many things on synthetic biology and disruptive technologies for the benefit of its readers. I believe that the successful commercialization of biotechnology requires a lot more than just ideas; it also requires an effective technology transfer system, including an investment community for disruptive technologies.

I greatly admire both of them for writing this beautiful book which can be used for any business.

Finally, I wish both of them to achieve their noble goal and I would like to invite the readers worldwide to get a copy of the book and not to miss the chance to read it.

Justin Roy E. Villa, MBA
Member, Team Perpetual Light Biotechnologies
Cebu City, Philippines
June, 2018

EPILOGUE

There is a future scenario we envision for the Bioluminescent Light (disruptive innovation of the future) which will have rural communities benefiting from our perpetual bioluminescent lighting product. I hope that this book will capture the readers' interest in this alternative renewable energy of the world that will be derived from the intersection of technology and biology.

I was very happy to be a part of the team, together with Justin Roy Villa who joined the IDE 2018 Accelerator Program in Thailand with Dr. Khanser and Dr. Soontorn, composing the Team Perpetual Light Biotechnologies for our product idea on perpetual light bioluminescent lighting system. We did interviews of potential customers during the training period.

I am also glad that Dr Soontorn and Dr. Khanser collaborated to write a book for the readers all over the world to understand the basic concepts of the phenomenon of bioluminescence and to get to know about the bioluminescent lighting system as a disruptive innovation. I admire their passion and ambitious goal. I should add that I hope they will receive a Nobel Prize in the future for their invention.

Finally, I would like to invite readers to read the book and to be inspired by the exciting ideas in the book, such as bioluminescence, synthetic biology, and Industry 4.0, among others.

Rita Dris Umali, MM
Member
Team Perpetual Light Biotechnologies
June, 2018

BIBLIOGRAPHY

BOOKS

Benyus, J. (1997). *Biomimicry: Innovation Inspired by Nature*. New York: William Morrow Paperbacks.

Brown, D. (2017). *Origin*. New York: Doubleday.

Brumet, R. (2010). *Birthing a Greater Reality: A Guide to Conscious Evolution*. Kansas, Missouri: Unity Books.

Darwin, C. (1859). *The Origin of Species*. New York: Penguin Books.

Duncan, C. (2016). *Alibaba: The House that Jack Ma Built*. New York: HarperCollins.

Foster, R. and Kaplan, S. (2001). *Creative Destruction: Why Companies that Are Built to Last Underperform the*

Market – and How to Successfully Transform Them. New York:Crown Business.

Haren, F. (2004). *The Idea Book.* Sweden: The Interesting Organization.

Harvey, N. E. (1957). *A History of Luminescence from the earliest times to 1900.* Philadelphia, USA: American Philosophical Society.

Hoffman, A. J. (1998). *Global Climate Change.* San Francisco, USA: The New Lexington Press.

Issacson, W. (2007). *Einstein: His Life and Universe.* New York: Simon & Schuster Paperbacks.

Issacson, W. (2011). *Steve Jobs.* New York: Simon & Schuster.

Kaku, M. (2011). *Physics of the Future: The Inventions that will Transform our Lives.* London: Penguin Books, Ltd.

Khanser, M.A. (2007). *John L. Gokongwei, Jr.: The Path of Entrepreneurship.* Quezon City, Philippines: Ateneo de Manila University.

Lee, J. (2016). *Bioluminescence: The Nature of the Light.* Georgia, USA: The University of Georgia.

Lee, J. (2017). *Basic Bioluminescence.* Georgia, USA: University of Georgia.

Lightman, A. (1993). *Einstein's Dreams.* New York: Warner Books Edition.

Myers, W. (2012). *Bio-Design: Nature + Science + Creativity.* New York: Museum of Modern Art.

Nissenson, H. (2001). *The Songs of the Earth.* Chapel Hill, North Carolina: Algonquin Books of Chapel Hill.

Schumpeter, J. A. (1934). *The Theory of Economic Development: An Inquiry into Profits, Capital, Credit, Interest, and the Business Cycle*. Cambridge, MA: Harvard University Press.

Redfield, J. (1999). *The Secret of Shambala: In Search of the Eleventh Insight*. New York: Grand Central Publishing.

Ries, E. (2017). *The Lean Startup*. New York: Currency.

Rowling, J.K. (2008). *Very Good Lives: The Fringe Benefits of Failure and the Importance of Imagination*. New York: Little, Brown and Company.

Starski, A. (2007). *Cold Light: Creatures, Discoveries, and Inventions that Glow*. Pennsylvania: Boyd Wills Press, Inc.

Tancharoen, A. (2009). *The common of an uncommon insect "firefly"*. Bangkok, Thailand: Kasetsart University.

Vance, A. (2015). *Elon Musk: Tesla, SpaceX, and the Quest for a Fantastic Future*. New York: ECCO.

Watson, J. (1968). *The Double Helix: A Personal Account of the Discovery of The Structure of DNA*. New York: The Atheneum Press.

Wilson, T. & Hastings, W. T. (2013). *Bioluminescence: Living Lights, Lights for Living*. New York: Harvard University Press.

JOURNAL ARTICLES

Atkinsons, et al. (1997). A Stakeholder's Approach to Strategic Performance Management. Cambridge, Massachusetts: *Sloan Management Review* Vol. 38, Issue 3.

Branchine, B. (2004). Chemistry of Firefly Bioluminescence. *Photobiology*.

Brumet, R. (2011). The Role of Technology in Spiritual Revolution. Kansas, Missouri: *Unity Books*.

Christensen, C. , Raynor, M., & McDonald, R. (2015). What is Disruptive Innovation? Cambridge, Mass: *Harvard Business Review.*

Chakaborty, D. & Roy, J. (2013). Corporate Carbon Footprint Accounting of an Indian Paper Board and Paper Production Unit. *International Journal of Insights & Transformation,* Vol. 6, Issue 1, Oct-March.

Cucek, L. et al., (2012). A Review of Footprint Analysis Tools for Monitoring Impacts on Sustainability. *Journal of Clean Production.* Vol. 34, pp 9-20.

Hastings, W. and Greenberg, E.P. (1999). Quorum Sensing: the Experiment of a Curious Phenomenon Reveals a Common Characteristic of Bacteria. *Journal of Bacteriology,* 181 (9).

Hoffert, M. I. (2002). Advanced Technology Paths to Global Climate Stability: Energy for a Greenhouse Planet. *Science,* Vol. 298, Issue 5595, pp 981-987.

Jay, S., Jones, C., Slinn, P. and Wood, C. (2007). Environmental impact assessment: Retrospect and prospect.

Environmental Impact Assessment Review, Volume 27, issue 4.

Khanser, M. and Racaza, C. (2017). Measuring Carbon Trading and Footprint of Selected Companies in Southeast Asia. Malaysia: *CIMA Voice.*

McElroy, W. (1982). William McElroy and the Illuminating Story of Bioluminescence. *Essays of an Information Scientist,* Vol. 5.

McElroy, W. (1947). The Energy Source for Bioluminescence in an Isolated System. *Proceedings from the National Academy of Science,* Nv. 33 (11) 342-3.

McElroy, W. D., Seliger, H.H. and White, E. H. (1969). Mechanism of Bioluminescence, Chemi-lumiescence and Enzyme Function in the Oxidation of Firefly Luciferin. Hanover, New Hampshire: *Symposium on Bioluminescence, Fifth International Congress on Photo-biology.*

Ratnunga, J. (2008). Carbonomics: Strategic Management Accounting Issues. *Journal of Applied Management Accounting Research* (JAMAR)., Vol. 6, No. 1

Sarkis, J., Hervani, A. and Helms, M. (2005). Performance Measurement for Green Supply Chain Management. *Benchmarking: An International Journal,* 12, 330-353.

Vierra, S. (2011). Biomimicry: Designing to Model Nature. *Institute of Building Science.*

Widder, E. A.(2014). Review of Bioluminescence for Engineers and Scientists in Biophotonics. Biophotonic Reviews.

Widder, E.A. (2010). Bioluminescence in the Ocean: Origins of Biological, Chemical, and Ecological Diversity. Science, Vol. 328, 7 May.

Wilson, T. and Hastings, J. W. (2013). Bioluminescence: living lights, lights for Living. Cambridge, MA.: Harvard University Press.

UNPUBLISHED MATERIALS

Lloyds' Emerging Risks Team Report (2009). *Synthetic Biology Influencing Development.* July, 2009.

World Economic Forum (2018). *The Next Economic Growth Engine: Scaling Fourth Industry Revolution Technologies in Production.* Geneva, Switzerland.

Hansen, M. B. (2010). *Disruptive Innovations and Business Models. Master Thesis.* International Business Economics.

ACKNOWLEDGMENTS

The publication of this book would not have been possible without the help and support of so many individuals and institutions, and we would like to thank and acknowledge them, as follows:

We express our heartfelt appreciation and thanks to **Professor Worsak Kanok-Nukulchai, PhD** (UC Berkeley), President of Asian Institute of Technology, Bangkok, Thailand, for the Foreword that he prepared for our book; we are greatly honored by this opportunity.

We are very grateful for the Foreword prepared for us by **Mr. Edmundo Isidro,** President of **Philippine Venture Capital Investment Group** (Philvencap). This was the group that first listened to the pitch we made about the perpetual lighting system using bioluminescence on October 26, 2017. We thank the Philvencap deeply for the opportunity to present our product idea to their investing audience.

Dr. Edith Ridder, the President of Ocean Research & Conservation Association, Inc., Duerr Laboratory for Marine Conservation, Florida, USA. We would like to express our gratitude and appreciation for her article on marine bioluminescence that she shared with us; it helped us understand the behavior of light emitting marine organisms. It has been a great honor for us to have known her since we know she is the world expert on marine bioluminescence.

Dr. Anchana Thancharoen, of the Department of Entomology, Faculty of Agriculture, Kasetsart University, Bangkok, Thailand. We are so grateful for her sharing of her time and expertise during the interview conducted in Bangkok, in April 2018, by Dr. Soontorn Piromsartkoon, one of the authors of this book. With her permission, we have included the results of the interview in Chapter 10 of this book.

We wish to thank the **IDE 2018 Accelerator Program of Thailand and MIT-Boston** that admitted us, the Team Perpetual Light Biotechnologies, to the accelerator. In particular, we thank **Dr. Edward Rubesch**, IDE Center Accelerator Program Director, for his guidance and support as we struggled to clarify our product idea on the perpetual lighting system using bioluminescence, and for imparting to us the 24 Steps of Disciplined Entrepreneurship of MIT-Boston, USA. We would also like to thank our coaches and mentors for our consultations with them during the IDE Accelerator meetings at UTCC, Bangkok, Thailand. We thank Dr. Rubesch for declaring our team's product idea as one of the few deserving of the Best Idea Award.

We would like to thank **Br. Romualdo Abulad, SVD,** for his excellent editing of our book to ensure that it is free of grammar and technical errors in order to achieve quality of the content.

Our gratitude and thanks to **Justin Roy Villa** and **Rita Umali,** members of our Team Perpetual Light Biotechnologies, as part of the Fellows that were admitted to join the IDE 2018 Accelerator Program of UTCC, Thailand and MIT-Boston, USA, from November, 2017 to March, 2018. During the preparations of the product concept, both Justin and Rita were very helpful. Thank you from the bottom of our hearts. It was a journey that was worth undertaking. Thank you also for your Epilogues.

We thank **Central Books** for their support in the printing and publication of our book, especially to Elaine, for the assistance. We thank our co-publisher, the executives and staff of **Mentor Management Consultant Company (MMC), Ltd,** in Bangkok, Thailand, for all the support.

We appreciate the beautiful book cover design prepared by our graphic artist, **Brendon Baclaan.**

We also thank our layout artist, **Edik Dolotina,** from F.F. Sibi Printing Press, from Cebu City, for the layout of this book, and **Louie Rizarri,** for his support.

We would like to thank the **administrators of the School**

of Business and Economics (SBE) of the **University of San Carlos** for their moral support while we were writing this book; our thanks also to all the colleagues of Dr. Khanser, from SBE, in particular the **BA Department,** for the challenge they posed on us to prove that our "crazy" idea was worth pursuing. We would like to thank the **SBE Dean, Dr. Challoner Matero;** the **Assistant Dean, Dr. Melanie de Ocampo; BA Chair Engr. Jovenal Arnaiz;** and SBE graduate program coordinator, **Dr. Larry Silapan.** Also, thanks to all the graduate students of Dr. Khanser for their support and enthusiasm for our product idea.

Finally, Dr. Soontorn would like to thank his parents for the talents and all the knowledge from the past.

And Dr. Khanser gives thanks to her **Papa,** aged 91, and her siblings; to the peer reviewer of this book: **Milagros Guerrero Barretto,** representing ordinary reader; likewise, to her thousands of students who await this book's publication.

Finally, and very importantly, we would like to thank our readers who will have our book in the future to understand the phenomenon of bioluminescence. We take responsibility for any mistakes that we may have unwittingly made in the book and give the assurance that we will correct them in the revised edition.

ILLUSTRATION CREDITS

1. On Page 34, photo provided by Thanakorn staff.

2. On Page 41, photo of solar panel as renewable energy. Photo taken by Dr. Soontorn Piromsartkoon, May 1, 2018.

3. On Page 42, photos of windmills, in Ranot, Songkhla, Thailand, as a renewable energy. Photo taken by Dr. Soontorn Piromsartkoon, May 1, 2018.

4. On Page 52, an illustration of an imagined street lighted by the GlowGlobe perpetual bioluminescent lamps. Graphic design concept by Brendon Baclaan.

5. On Page 60, a sketch of the light of a firefly being mimicked as a source of living light for a home. Sketch concept by Brendon Baclaan.

6. On Page 62, illustration of an imagined room being lighted by the GlowGlobe perpetual bioluminescent lighting system as lamps and a bio light panel. Graphic design concept by Brendon Baclaan.

7. On Page 85, close up photo of a firefly in the Firefly Learning Center, Kasertsat University, Bangkok, Thailand. Photo courtesy of Dr. Anchana Thancharoen, April 4, 2018.

8. On Page 86, photo of a firefly field with swarms of fireflies during evening. Photo courtesy by Dr. Anchana Thancharoen, April 4, 2018, Bangkok, Thailand.

9. On Page 90, the book of Dr. Anchana Tancharoen in Thai language version, titled, The Common of an Uncommon Insect "firefly" (Thancharoen, 2009). Photo by Edik Dolotina.

10. On Page 92, photo of Dr. Soontorn Piromsartkoon interviewing Dr. Anchana Thancharoen regarding fireflies, April 4, 2018, in Bangkok, Thailand. Photo taken by Dr. Soontorn.

11. On Page 127, photo of Namchok Petsaen, Chief Technology Officer and Co-founder of Toechok Co,. LTD, in Bangkok, Thailand. Photo taken by Dr. Soontorn Piromsartkoon, May 4, 2018.

12. On Page 157, photo of Dr. Soontorn Piromsartkoon with Prof. Worsak, President of AIT, in Bangkok, Thailand. Photo taken by AIT staff.

13. On Page 162, photo of Dr. Marites A. Khanser, holding the placard for winning for her team The Best Idea Award from IDEA 2018 Accelerator of Thailand and MIT-Boston, USA, during the November 26, 2017 first session in Bangkok, Thailand. Photo taken by IDE staff, November 26, 2017, Bangkok, Thailand.

14. On Page 169, illustrations of an imagined molecular biology laboratory where the GlowGlobe perpetual bioluminescent light is being developed as a prototype, and, an imagined office being lighted by the GlowGlobe perpetual bioluminescent light as ceiling bio lamps. Graphic design concept by Brendon Baclaan.

DECODING THE SECRETS OF CRETE

By **MARITES A. KHANSER, DBA**
AND
SOONTORN PIROMSARTKOON, DBA

A LOST CODEX, A HIDDEN PHARAOH'S TOMB

Somewhere in the heart of Tel-el-Amarna, the ancient city of Pharaoh Akhenaten in Central Egypt, lies hidden for millennia, a valuable codex. This is the lost codex that will unlock the enigma of the Phaistos disk]found in Crete in 1908 by Dr. Luigi Pernier, an eminent Italian archaeologist.

But how to find it?

This is Dr. Ulma Athena Davanis' quest as she travels from Manila in Southeast Asia to the Mediterranean Crete, and then to Central Egypt, in search of the missing codex. Two opposing forces though are preventing Dr. Davanis from finding the lost codex.

The Lost Disk by **Marites Khanser** and **Soontorn Piromsartkoon** is a novel of suspense that will grip the readers and bring them to the ancient land of the Minoans, to Amarna in ancient Egypt, and finally, to the Phaistos Palace ruins. Will the codex be found or remain buried in the Amarna sands forever? This historical fiction tackles the current forgery controversy surrounding the Phaistos Disk, an ancient treasure of Greece.

Don't Fear
to Generate New Ideas
Advice for the Young Generation

By SOONTORN PIROMSARTKOON, DBA

In this new book, Dr. Soontorn Piromsartkoon advises the young generation of the world not to be afraid to generate new ideas for possible startups.

The world is changing so fast and so many great ideas are being offered that exciting business opportunities are coming as never before imagined. There are now many inventions that can be developed based on advanced information technology, changing the way we think of the computers that link us to the Internet. Dr. Soontorn would like to encourage young people to be more creative, imaginative, and innovative, as well as to take risks with their new ideas. He would like them to explore possible inventions for the future in the areas of biotechnology, artificial intelligence, machine learning, synthetic biology, nanotechnology, and space exploration, among others.

This is a book that challenges the young generation to handle the resistance that other people might have for their novel ideas. Others might not understand precisely because their ideas belong to the future. As Henry Ford famously said, "Whether you think you can, or think you can't, you're right. Believe that you can succeed, and you'll find ways through different obstacles. If you don't, you'll just find excuses."

Understanding
Conflict of Interest
Search for a New Model

By SOONTORN PIROMSARTKOON, DBA

This book attempts to provide readers with a deeper understanding of the social phenomenon of conflict of interest and how best to handle conflict of interest situations for the ethics of the professions such as lawyers, doctors, accountants, teachers, and engineers, and other medical practitioners. The author, Dr. Soontorn Piromsartkoon, presents cases drawn from different sectors of world societies where conflict of interest becomes the source of corruption.

The goal of the author is to propose a new management model of dealing with conflict of interest situations in order to lessen the occurrences of corruption that undermine the moral fiber of modern society.

World eco-tourism is about sustainability in the global tourism business through policy-making, planning and regulation, product development, marketing and promotion. It is also a tool for the economic development of countries which have the natural resources much sought after by world tourists. This book, which promises economically sustainable business through a well-managed world eco-tourism, thus strikes a balance between profit and the sustainability of the world's protected ecosystems.

The author laments that our world today is in pain because of the rampant destruction of the environment in the name of profit. In this book, he enjoins everyone to stop the devastation of the only world we have. The solution to this problem, according to him, is an effective world eco-tourism management.

Marites A. Khanser, DBA, presents in this book the research findings, insights, and lessons learned from the empirical research studies conducted by her graduate students on various aspects of Knowledge Management (KM). Dr. Khanser uses an Asian Approach in developing a Knowledge Management Process Framework useful for organizations in an Asian setting.

Dr. Khanser focuses on organizational knowledge as a source of competitive advantage of firms and how they can leverage and improve company performance through Knowledge Creation and Acquisition, Knowledge Codification, and Knowledge Transfer. Readers will learn the best practices in all aspects of managing organizational knowledge.

Marites A. Khanser, DBA, has been teaching Knowledge Management in Philippine universities for the past 15 years and has mentored graduate students in their Knowledge Management research projects. Dr. Khanser is an international researcher, a book author and Management Consultant for industry clients. She finished a Doctor of Business Administration from the De La Salle University, Manila, in 1998. She is the author of the business biography, John L. Gokongwei, Jr.: The Path of Entrepreneurship, published by the Ateneo de Manila University in 2007.

APPENDICES

Appendix A

INTERVIEW PROTOCOL FOR DR. ANCHANA
BY DR. SOONTORN PIROMSARTKOON

Guide Questions:

On your 16 years of study on fireflies

1. You have made a great contribution to the advancement on the understanding of the nature of fireflies. Tell us about how you got interested on the study of fireflies as entymologist.

2. What are some of the important findings you made on your firefly research.

3. Can you tell us the evolutionary origins of fireflies as bioluminescent organism. What insights did you learn in terms of the survival of the bioluminescent fireflies over the long term?

On bioluminescence technology

4. We are writing a book, titled, *Bioluminescent Light: A Disruptive Innovation of the Future* (Khanser and Piromsartkoon, 2018). We would like to know your opinion on making use of the phenomenon of bioluminescence as an alternative source of light for humans. We are talking here of biotechnology and synthetic biology as the process of coming up with products using bioluminescence.

5. What benefits can you foresee for those who are developing lighting systems using bioluminescence as the source of light and what is your opinion of this development in biotechnology and synthetic biology, i.e. coming up with glowing trees, or lighting systems that can be a form of green energy?

6. What in your opinion are the risks related to biological use of light for commercial products to be used by humans as an alternative energy to light their homes, offices and streets?

7. We envision bioluminescent lighting system as a disruptive innovations of the future. What are its cost implications in its development and how can its benefits outweigh its cost of production?

8. We are one of the few innovators in the world that are coming up with lighting system using bioluminescence inspired by the light of the fireflies. What do you think are our chances of succeeding in this invention?

9. What advice can you give us regarding our desire to mimic the light of the firefly using synthetic biology, and in general, biotechnology?

10. As a seasoned expert on fireflies, what is the future of these creators of light in the natural world in the face of pollution and global climate change? What steps can we make to ensure the long term survival of our bioluminescent organisms like fireflies, glowworms, and algae? Tell us about your role in protecting these creatures of living light which are illuminating our world.

Thank you very much for your time.

Appendix B

A Beautiful World

Lyrics and Music by Soontorn Piromsartkoon (2018)

i

When I was born, I saw a beautiful world
and the world consisted of wide expanse of land
Rain forests abound, animals roamed free
The ocean and sea creatures lived side by side
And the people lived in harmony
Together and free and loved one another.

ii

When this time was gone
And I was young, and I
saw many people
destroyed this world
By killing animals and cutting the trees in the forests
and making an atomic bomb
To kill the world and Make the world so warm
by industrialization and by what is called progress.

(Refrain)

Like today. The world is crying and in pain
caused by earthquakes, hurricanes,and storms
please let us stop destroying of the world.

iii
We are the people and
We have a responsibility for the World
we must cleanse the world by
Keeping the balance of Nature
And stop the
Killing by our Hand
Of the people in the world. .

vi
We are the people,
we must keep a beautiful world
Maintain its natural environment
Let us stop destroying
the only World we have. (2X)

(Repeat Refrain)

GLOSSARY OF TERMS

Abstract. This is one of the steps in the Biomimicry Design Spiral. It requires that we get the essence or we distill nature's principles that are at work in our design.

Accelerator. This refers to business incubation wherein individuals are provided with training and hands-on skills to develop their business ideas.

Adenosine Triphosphate (ATP). This is an energy storing molecule found in all living cells, which is required for the emission of light; the amount of light is directly proportional to the amount of ATP.

Allied Services. This refers to other similar services that can be offered outside of the mainstream. For instance, in digital technology, services need to be provided to make the technology work.

Ancient Memory. This pertains to long term memory, even as far back as the ancient past.

Artificial Intelligence. This refers to the robotics technologies that are expected to soon surpass human intelligence in terms of highly quantitative tasks. These robots are also able to come closer to speech recognition and are able to perform repetitive tasks in the manufacturing sector.

Bargaining Power of Buyers. This refers to one of the competitive forces under Porter's Model in which buyers are able to choose products that offer them more value for their money. Such can affect the price of products.

Bargaining Power of Suppliers. This refers to the ability of suppliers to make their own demands on companies that need their products or services. They can raise the price of raw materials or refuse to supply certain companies if their offer is not competitive.

Beagle. This refers to the vessel used by Charles Darwin as he studied the behavior of species in Galapagos Island and which became the basis of his book, *The Origin of Species*. It was Darwin who developed the theory of the survival of the fittest.

Big Data. This refers to the properties of "Big Data" that have been included as "5Vs theory"; the most famous 3Vs are volume, variety, and velocity, which were introduced by

Gartner analyst Laney (200). Volume refers to the large amount of data, while variety refers to the great number of types of data including weblog, music, video, picture, geographical position, etc. Lastly, velocity refers to the high speed of data process, which is the most distinct feature of the traditional databases which are being used for decision making. These data come from such social media as Facebook and Twitter, among others.

Biodegradable. This is one classification of waste segregation, where waste is turned into biomass. Waste such as food waste and others can be used for the production of biofuels.

Biodesign. This has specifically to do with living organisms as essential components of design, thus the need of design artists to collaborate with biologists and other scientists.

Biological Evolution. This traces the evolutionary history of the Earth.

Bioluminescence. This is visible light made by organisms. In the context of biophotonics, the light may be emitted by organisms, such as bacteria, or by light-producing chemicals extracted from bioluminescent organisms. The light it emits is "cold light" as opposed to thermal light which is hot.

Bioluminescent Imaging (BLI). This technique allows for the noninvasive imaging of biological processes in living animals.

Among other uses, this makes it possible to study the processes of various diseases and of treatments for those diseases. It can also be used to locate tumors.

Bioluminescent Light. This is light created by some light emitting species through some kind of chemical reaction in their body. For instance, fireflies are able to emit light through a chemical reaction in which luciferin is converted to oxyluciferin by the luciferase enzyme. These are the chemicals produced by the fireflies in their bodies. The luciferin is the key to the emission of light by certain organisms. It needs of course oxygen to combine with for the chemical reaction to take place.

Bioluminescent Resonance Energy Transfer (BRET). This is used to map neuronal circuits in order to understand brain function.

Biomass. It is produced when organic wastes, such as trees, wood wastes and agriculture residues decay. For example, landfills offer a primary source of biomass. This can be converted to fuel through combustion for the generation of electricity. The resulting gas is methane and can be used as an alternative energy.

Biomimicry. It is defined by Benyus (1997) as "the science and art of emulating Nature's best biological ideas to solve human problems." This looks at nature for solutions to human problems and learn from it.

Biomimicry Design Spiral. This refers to the Biomimicry process that Benyus (1997) developed consisting of the following: identify, interpret, discover, abstract, emulate, evaluate, and identify, and then the loop begins again. This is useful when using Biomimicry design project.

Biotechnology. This refers to a technology that is combined with biology. In other words, it is technology based on biology. Biotechnology makes use of cellular and biomolecular processes to develop technologies and products.

Business Ideas. These refer to raw ideas that have been selected for their business potential.

Capability Deprivation. This refers to condition of the poor people all over the world, people who have not been given the capability and skills to rise from poverty. They are thus deprived of the ability to improve their lives.

Carbon Emission Credits. These are tradeable assets given as incentives to companies that reduce their carbon emission which then can be traded in carbon trading exchanges or in voluntary offset markets.

Carbon Footprint. This is a measure of the total amount of carbon dioxide emissions that is directly or indirectly caused by or accumulated over the life cycle stages of a product.

Carbon Price. This refers to the price that firms which have high GHG emissions need to pay per tonne of the carbon dioxide (CO2) that they are emitting in the environment. This strategy of attaching a price to carbon emissions and creating a market to trade them is done to give incentives to those companies which have reduced their carbon footprint.

Carbon Trading. This refers to a market-based mechanism by which to mitigate the negative impact of climate change. It allows companies to earn emission credits if they have reduced their carbon emissions. These carbon credits can be traded in carbon trading exchanges or in voluntary offset markets. Carbon trading is one of the mechanisms to encourage companies to reduce their carbon emissions by engaging in carbon trading activities.

Chemiluminescence. This is light produced through chemical reaction.

Clean Development Mechanism (CDM). This comprises renewable energy, clean energy program and other mechanisms to combat global climate change.

Climate Change Mitigation. It offers solutions to address the global climate change which are activities that reduce GHG emissions, such as carbon dioxide reduction or carbon footprint reduction. There is an international collaboration of various stakeholders to come up with solutions to reduce the negative effects of global warming and ozone depletion. In the context of climate change, mitigation is defined as a human intervention to reduce the sources or enhance the sinks of greenhouse gases (GHGs).

Cold Light. It is defined as the chemistry of animals and things that make light but not heat (Starski, 2007). Bioluminescent organisms emit cold light, which is only 20% thermal heat. This type of heat results from a specific biochemical mechanism involving chemical processes, often specific for that organism. The cold light in bioluminescent systems is generated by a chemical reaction and is therefore a form of chemiluminescence, hence produced by chemical reaction.

Corporate Social Responsibility. This is a commitment of a company to contribute to the social development of communities by engaging in activities that will improve the quality of life of the residents.

Creative Destruction. This process pertains to the never-ending cycle of creation and destruction of enterprises across markets and industries. This means that the innovative companies simultaneously create new products and business models and eliminate others.

Culture of Science. This pertains to the academic atmosphere necessary for the young science-inclined students to nurture their love for science and technology so they can pursue scientific careers. This culture will drive inventions and innovations since new ideas will come from the young, given the right training and motivation for excellence.

Disruptive Designs. These are the products developed by disruptive innovators.

Disruptive Innovation. This pertains to how innovators disrupt the market by introducing products and services that are not as good as the current products and they do not aim to bring better products to high-end customers. However, when they move from low- end market to high end, disruption happens.

Disruptors. Under disruptive innovation model, the disruptors are the individuals who adopt disruptive innovation so as to introduce it in the low end market segment. They make changes and transformations and compete with the more stable companies by offering products that are easy to use, and cheaper yet.

Energy Field. This pertains to certain levels of energy that Buddhists are able to generate by observing certain steps to reach the highest energy level.

Entomologist. This refers to an individual who is an expert on a particular insect, such as the firefly. The scientist spends considerable years of study and devotes his/her career on the study of this particular species.

Environmental Havoc. This refers to the environmental damage caused by global climate change. The havoc can be in the form of natural disasters such as typhoons, earthquakes, hurricanes, and storm surges, among others.

Environmental Impact Assessment. This is the tool being used in the United States to assess the impact of a project on environment and health.

Flashing Behavior. This refers to the capacity of bioluminescent organisms like fireflies to emit flashing light for mating purposes.

Flexible Automation. This incorporates response mechanisms, automation and remote movement. This also pertains to automation technology in the manufacturing sector.

Fireflies. These insects belong to the family of beetles called Lampyridae as its scientific name. For some scientists, they are better known as lightning bugs. Fireflies emit light called bioluminescent light in their bodies through chemical reaction. These are terrestrial bioluminescent species and they are the most studied by researchers doing work on bioluminescence.

Fourth Industrial Revolution. This is the next economic engine and it focuses on technology and innovation for the future of production.

Frontiers of Science. This refers to scientific inventions that are pioneering and cannot still be understood by many people today.

Genetic Manipulation. The essence is that new biological systems and organisms are created or designed by genetically engineering the DNA cells.

Gene Promoter. This is the invention based on the Green Fluorescent Protein (GFP) which won a Nobel Prize in 2008. It is a bio marker that is used to trace the presence of illnesses and diseases in the human body.

Global Climate Change. This refers to the phenomenon of both global warming and ozone depletion. The environmental degradation contributes to this change in the Planet. Increases in greenhouse effect are referred to as global warming or global climate change.

Green Business. This refers to doing business with concern for environmental protection. Companies that follow the green path are thus said to be doing green business.

Green Customers. These are customers that adopt the lifestyle of buying only from companies that are following the green path. They patronize products that are environment-friendly.

Green Energy. This refers to an environment-friendly energy source commonly known as Renewable Energy or Sustainable

Energy, which comes from a natural source like wind, water, and sunlight. Such green energy can be produced with little pollution, with less or no carbon footprint, so that it does not contribute to climate change or global warming. In this book's context, this refers to the bioluminescent lighting system that does not have carbon footprint.

Green Fluorescent Protein (GFP). This is a photoprotein which acts as biomarker. The remarkable brightly glowing green fluorescent protein was first observed in the beautiful jellyfish, Aequorea victoria in 1962. Since then, this protein has become one of the most important tools used in contemporary bioscience. This glowing marker allows medical professionals to watch the movements, positions and interactions of the tagged proteins. The three inventors of this biomarker won the Nobel Prize in 2008.

Green Supplier. This refers to suppliers who hold a certification that they are engaged in green business.

Host. This refers to the microorganism which is re-engineered to produce the chemical reaction that results in bioluminescent light. As genetically modified microorganism it is able to do something which does not belong to its nature.

Human Consciousness. This refers to the human soul that is borne out of human spirituality. This consciousness is higher than the consciousness of lower life forms such as plants and animals.

This makes humanity truly human because of the human soul.

Human Spiritual Evolution. This refers to the ability of humans to evolve into spiritual beings, thus achieving their full human potential.

Human Imagination. This refers to a human ability that cannot be matched by Artificial Intelligence. It is the ability to think of novel ideas that have never been heard before. Also, it the capacity to envision the future, to be creative and innovative by using one's mind.

Hydroelectric Power. This renewable energy harnesses water cycle, falling water, running water or ocean energy (power or waves) for useful purposes. A hydroelectric power station utilizes water flow to power a turbine. The turbines are connected to generators that produce energy through the use of water currents. The amount of energy generated is determined by the speed the water flows.

Industry 4.0. This is also called the Fourth Industrial Revolution. This is a new economic engine, driven by technology and innovation.

Innovation Chain Process. This process starts with early research, followed by demonstration and commercialization, when the new knowledge is applied to the real world; then it goes through piloting, demonstrating, and becoming a maiden commercial-scale project; the last step is market uptake.

Internet of Things (IoT). This is the term that refers to all forms of digital platforms. Online business, digital stores, and online shopping are some of the digital platforms that IoT enables and which depend largely on the Internet, thereby increasing connectivity, particularly in the production process. This online integration of processes from production to consumption shortens the lead time and enables faster production, likewise reaching consumers more quickly.

Inventions. These are products or services that are the results of a new discovery.

Landfill Gas. This refers to the waste material that is generated by human activities that ends up in a landfill where it decomposes and produces a gas mode of approximately 5% methane. This gas can be captured and used to fuel electric generators. Since large landfills must burn off this gas anyway in order to reduce the hazards arising from gas buildup, this method of renewable energy is one of the most successful.

Leaps of Intelligence. This refers to the ability of human intelligence to increase intelligence and creativity by leaps and bounds, or exponentially, which cannot be matched by Artificial Intelligence which is just a creation of humans.

Life Cycle Assessment (LCA). This is a tool that can be used to evaluate the carbon emissions of a product process or activity throughout its life cycle. It is also called "cradle to grave" approach since it traces the carbon activities of a company in its manufacturing process. It likewise .quantifies emissions, resource consumptions, and environmental and health impacts associated with processes, products, or activities throughout its life cycle. The LCA is comprised of four phases: goal and scope definition, inventory analysis, Life Impact Assessment (LIA), and interpretation.

Living Light. This refers to bioluminescent light.

Machine Learning. This refers to artificial neural networks, fuzzy logic, genetic algorithms, and other advanced financial technologies which aid companies in decision making.

Market Uptake. This is the last step in the innovation process when the disruptive product is proven commercially viable; when introduced to the market, it competes with the rest of the old products and disrupts their existence.

Multiverses. This refers to the possibility of having many universes, or multiple worlds outside of the Earth and in far galaxies. In quantum physics, this means many dimensions of the universe.

Nature-Inspired Innovation. These are creative designs like engineering designs and architectural designs, among others which are derived from learning from nature or mimicking nature.

New Entrants. In Porter's Five Forces Model, these are newcomers to the market that will pose as competitors together with their product offerings.

Non-Pathogenic. This refers to the microorganisms that will serve as host in the bioluminescent lighting system, which requires friendly microbes so as not to result in a pandemic or an epidemic or infections or other health problems.

Open Universities. This refers to schools that offer electronic learning or the online mode of delivery through the online platform. Students need not report to the physical classrooms because they can now get their training through the Internet technologies or virtual classrooms.

Ozone Depletion. This is a part of global warming that allows ultraviolet light through the atmosphere; the greenhouse effect warms the planet because the atmosphere spreads visible light over the earth's surface.

Quorum Sensing. This is a tool used to detect, at low cell densities, the luciferase gene which was not transcribed; however, luminescent genes do activate at high cell densities when the emitted light is bright enough to serve a purpose. It is now accepted that cell-cell communication in bacteria is common.

Perpetual Bioluminescent Lighting System. This is the invention being introduced in this book which pertains to the development of a lighting system that uses bioluminescence and produces perpetual or continuous living light. The technology innovators call their product GlowGlobe, based on their tagline "Glowing the Globe."

Pilot Purgatory. This is a phase in the Industry 4.0 where technology is deployed experimentally by companies at a reduced scale for an extended period due to the inability or lack of conviction to roll it out at production-system scale.

Prototype. In the stages of product development, this is the second stage after the business idea is implemented. This is a sample of the proposed product which is needed to find out if the product will work once introduced in the market.

Red Planet. This refers to the Planet Mars.

Renewable Energy. This pertains to alternative forms of energy to mitigate climate change, such as bio-energy, direct solar energy, geothermal energy, hydropower, ocean energy, and wind energy.

Rivalry among Firms. This is one of the competitive forces under Porter's model which refers to the presence of competing firms in an industry; such rivalry can be very competitive.

Shelf Life. This refers to the duration of the life of a product until their expiration, when they are no longer fit for consumption.

Solar Energy. This is made up of cells that convert sunlight to electricity without any moving parts. The conversion of sunlight into electricity is made possible by the special properties of a semi-conducting material.

Space Solar Power. This refers to the possible alternative energy coming from space. This will harness the power from the sun by putting up satellites in space so as to beam the sun's rays as microwave radiation that reaches the Planet Earth. It was Nikola Tesla, a world famous inventor, who first thought of the possibility of harnessing power from the sky.

Spiritual Beings. These pertain to the spiritual dimension of human beings, aside from their physical being.

Startup Costs. This pertains to the expenses that will be incurred when a new business venture, called a startup, is put up. This also pertains to the pre-operation costs such as developing the prototype.

Substitute Products. According to Porters' Five Forces Model, the substitute products that are introduced in the market will be a source of competition for the original product that they mean to substitute. These substitute products thus offer a choice to the customers.

Survival of the Fittest. This is derived from the book of Charles Darwin, *The Origin of Species* (1859), where he observed through his research that there is a rule that prevails among creatures of the Earth, where the strongest, the fittest and the ablest survive and the weak and unfit are eliminated.

Sustaining Innovation. This type of innovation has the company aiming at very demanding high-end customers and what the company does is to improve on the products and continuously engage in incremental improvements year by year.

Symbiotic Relationship. This refers to the presence of bioluminescent bacteria in some marine species; the glow of the bacteria enables the organism to defend itself from predators. Such bioluminescent bacteria is able to find a place for its growth by attaching itself to the marine organism.

Synthetic Biology. This refers to the application of engineering principles to biology in order to design and construct novel and biological systems for specific applications.

Technological Breakthroughs. These are inventions that are based on and driven by advances in technology.

Technology Innovators. These are the individuals and entrepreneurs who develop products and services that are technology-based.

Technological Progress. This refers to advancement of humankind through the technological breakthroughs that make modern life far more advanced than in the past.

Teleportation. This refers to the ability of the mind over matter. This means that the mind can move an object from Point A to Point B with just cognitive suggestion.

Threat of New Entrants. This refers to the entrance of new companies as new competitors that will challenge existing companies in an industry.

Threat of Substitute Products. This refers to products that can replace a similar product that is gaining the upperhand, but customers can shift from the current product when there are available substitute products which offer a cheaper price or a better choice in terms of product quality.

Venture Capital Funding. This is the financing that comes from venture capitalists, angel investors, and financing institutions; this is provided to promising startups so they can develop their prototype or develop their business ideas into commercial products.

Venture Capital Industry. This refers to the presence of an industry composed of venture capitalists, angel investors, businessmen, entrepreneurs, and financial institutions that finance new venture creations or startups to enable the innovators to survive financially in the early stages of their business development.

Voluntary Offset Market. This is a carbon trading exchange where companies trade their carbon emission credits with those willing to buy them; the offset will work as carbon tax exemption.

Water Environment. In a futuristic submerged world, most cities will have water environment; these cities will be submerged in water.

Wind. It is defined as a current of air (sometimes with considerable force) from an area of high pressure to an area of low pressure. The beam of the radiation from the sun would heat the Earth's surface and creates temperature differences between the land, water, and air due to their different properties, such as density, which affect their respective abilities to absorb heat. All these temperature differences and properties create what we know as wind.

Workplace. This is the location where employees work. It can be a physical workplace or a virtual workplace.

INDEX

A

J

K

L

P

Q

R

T

U